The Ethics of Disruption in Business

The Ethics of Disruption in Business

Contributions from Design Thinking and Catholic Social Thought

STEPHANIE ANN PUEN

◆PICKWICK *Publications* • Eugene, Oregon

THE ETHICS OF DISRUPTION IN BUSINESS
Contributions from Design Thinking and Catholic Social Thought

Copyright © 2024 Stephanie Ann Puen. All rights reserved. Except for brief quotations in critical publications or reviews, no part of this book may be reproduced in any manner without prior written permission from the publisher. Write: Permissions, Wipf and Stock Publishers, 199 W. 8th Ave., Suite 3, Eugene, OR 97401.

Pickwick Publications
An Imprint of Wipf and Stock Publishers
199 W. 8th Ave., Suite 3
Eugene, OR 97401

www.wipfandstock.com

PAPERBACK ISBN: 978-1-6667-8556-2
HARDCOVER ISBN: 978-1-6667-8557-9
EBOOK ISBN: 978-1-6667-8558-6

Cataloguing-in-Publication data:

Names: Puen, Stephanie Ann, author.

Title: The ethics of disruption in business : contributions of design thinking and Catholic social thought / Stephanie Ann Puen.

Description: Eugene, OR : Pickwick Publications, 2024 | Includes bibliographical references.

Identifiers: ISBN 978-1-6667-8556-2 (paperback) | ISBN 978-1-6667-8557-9 (hardcover) | ISBN 978-1-6667-8558-6 (ebook)

Subjects: LCSH: Catholic Church—Doctrines. | Economics—Religious aspects—Catholic Church. | Christian sociology—Catholic Church | Product design.

Classification: BX1795.E27 .P78 2024 (print) | BX1795.E27 .P78 (ebook)

Table of Contents

Acknowledgments vii
Introduction ix

Chapter 1: The Challenge of Wicked Problems in Business 1
    Structures of Sin in Catholic Social Thought and Theology 1
    Structures of Sin in Business Ethics 21
    Wicked Problems 23
    Conclusion: Structures of Sin as Wicked Problems in Business as
        Opportunities for Disruption 30

Chapter 2: Business and Business Ethics in Catholic Social Thought 33
    Business Ethics-Related Principles and Themes in Magisterial
        Documents 34
    Business Ethics-Related Principles and Themes in Select Catholic
        Theologians' Work 49
    Key Themes in Catholic Social Thought 51
    Conclusion: Principles of Catholic Social Thought as Disruption 54

Chapter 3: Responding to Wicked Problems with Design Thinking 57
    Design Thinking 58
    Design Thinking Principles 63
    Critiques of Design Thinking 70
    The Value of Dialogue between Design Thinking and Theology as
        Method for Disruption 73
    Conclusion: Design Thinking as a Methodology for Disruption 76

TABLE OF CONTENTS

Chapter 4: Design Thinking and Catholic Social Thought: A Dialogue for Disruption 78
    Points of Dialogue 79
    Contributions of Design Thinking and Catholic Social Thought to Business Ethics 92
    Catholic Social Thought's Contribution to Design Thinking 95
    Conclusion: Concretely Synthesizing Design Thinking and Catholic Social Thought for Ethical Disruption 98

Chapter 5: An Ethic of Disruption towards Structures of Grace 100
    Structures of Grace 102
    The Business Value Chain and Business Model as a Structure of Grace 125
    Conclusion: Ethical Disruption Using Design Thinking and Catholic Social Thought 134

Conclusion: Disrupting Structures and Moving Forward 137

Bibliography 143

Acknowledgments

First, thank *you* for picking up this work! I hope something in this book sparks reflection and engagement in how people grapple with and handle the complexities of the business world, given one's faith commitment.

I am grateful to my dissertation adviser, Dr. Christine Firer Hinze, and dissertation committee, Dr. Christiana Zenner, Fr. Thomas Massaro, SJ, Dr. Cristina Traina, and Fr. Bryan Massingale, for all the support and comments that have helped me shaped this into a book.

I am also grateful to the Ateneo de Manila University for their support in giving me time and resources to get this book out into the world. I am especially grateful for my colleagues in the Department of Theology, whose scholarship and friendship have been great resources for my work.

Lastly, I am thankful for my husband Miko, who is the epitome of joy and hope in the world, and whose infectious laughter gets me through everything and anything.

Introduction

DISRUPTION THEORY ITSELF, DISCUSSED as early as the mid-1990s, is the process wherein a smaller company with fewer resources is able to successfully challenge bigger and more established businesses in a particular industry. They often target overlooked segments with better products and services at an affordable price, then work their way up through the various markets in the industry.[1] Scholar Clayton Christensen explored how businesses might fail, not because they were making bad decisions. In fact, they kept making good decisions that kept the business going in the market. However, businesses were busy pleasing their current customers that they failed to notice and tap into other market segments with new products, services, or business models, many of which eventually took over the entire industry or system.[2]

Disruption is a concept that businesses use to describe the kind of groundbreaking work they would like to do to succeed. Facebook's Mark Zuckerberg popularized the phrase "move fast and break things" to capture this way of rapidly designing and conceptualizing products, services, and the ways in which business is conducted. The idea was to come up with a product or service or business model that would "disrupt" or drastically transform the way a particular industry worked. For some time, this mantra became the banner under which many businesses worked, especially in the wake of the success of "disruptors" such as Uber and Airbnb.[3]

The use of "disruption" as a buzzword has elicited challenges from scholars and businesspeople alike on the definition of disruption and whether companies, such as Uber and Airbnb, are true disruptors. They

1. Christensen et al., "What Is Disruptive Innovation?"
2. Clayton, *Innovators' Dilemma*.
3. For examples of analyses behind the success of Uber and Airbnb, see Bellissimo-Magrin, "How the Disruptive Uber Business Model"; Guttentag, "Airbnb," 1192–217.

Introduction

also began questioning what disruption genuinely means, given a society that is becoming more concerned about social issues such as environmental degradation, poverty, lack of healthcare and education, and businesses needing to once again adapt and nuance the kind of disruption they aim to do. Some scholars and businesspeople have also begun specifying what perhaps nondisruptive creation and growth might look like—where there is the "creation of a brand new market outside or beyond existing industry boundaries" that then becomes a space for businesses to respond to the needs of the people and enabling a business to prosper as well.[4] The questions asked included, "what systemic, societal change do you aspire to create with your product? How will you sustain the virtue of your product? How will [the business] keep [itself] accountable as [it] scale[s]? What framework does [the business] use for leveraging data and AI responsibly?" These are questions that businesses need to raise, given that they usually rely on having the minimum viable product or service to survive.[5]

"Moving fast and breaking things" thus takes on new meanings, and is no longer about getting the fastest product out there to be able to achieve what businesses call "first mover advantage." This is where businesses, the first entrants into a particular segment or industry, can claim a huge portion of the market and achieve certain benefits—no matter what the cost. Disruption will also mean two things: the speed at which products and services arrive at the market, and the ability "to explore multiple domains at once and combine them into something that produces value. We'll need computer scientists working with cancer scientists, for example, to identify specific genetic markers that could lead to a cure. To do this, we'll need to learn how to go slower to have a greater impact."[6]

In order to run businesses ethically and seek to disrupt the way business is currently practiced, "without leaving failed companies, lost jobs, and destroyed markets in its wake," paying attention to changing cultures and structures, and to the system and power dynamics involved are crucial.[7] Studies have shown that while people agree that ethical decisions are important to make in their economic and business dealings, they often fail to translate their desires and convictions into ethical decisions. This is so for a variety of reasons, including the way the systems that their business

---

4. Kim and Renée, *Beyond Disruption*, 13.
5. Taneja, "Era of 'Move Fast and Break Things' is Over."
6. Satell, *Why 'Move Fast and Break Things' Doesn't Work Anymore*.
7. Kim and Renée, *Beyond Disruption*, 7.

INTRODUCTION

comprises or is embedded in are set up. In the area of ethical consumption, for instance, many consumers might agree in surveys that food companies should behave ethically (i.e., sustainable, engage in such initiatives such as Fair Trade that compensate workers fairly). Yet frequently, there is a disconnect between this thinking and attitude, and the actual decisions people make about patronizing ethical products or services.[8] This disconnect can be for a number of reasons, such as: 1) price and convenience play a role and become the primary criteria in consumer decisions, especially for those who are not as well off; 2) limits to consumers' purchasing power because of the way salaries and compensation are structured; 3) even when consumers have some purchasing power to decide where to spend their money, their purchasing power is limited by information asymmetry (i.e., the consumer lacks the information needed to determine whether the company, product or service is truly ethical); or 4) other aspects of business and economics that tend to skew the power toward bigger organizations, which have the resources and manpower to affect consumer behavior more than vice versa.

Addressing these challenges, business ethicist and philosopher Oscar Bulaong emphasizes the importance of integrating systems thinking into business ethics and business ethics education. This is crucial in order to help students think not only of individual ethical action, but also the complex relations that they are dealing with when making ethical business decisions.[9] Another example is theological ethicist Joerg Rieger, who argues in his work on religion, economics, and empire that people need to pay attention to the ways the global economic system has disproportionately negatively affected less powerful groups of people. Rieger points out that "what should give [people] pause is that, despite a virtually ideal situation for the free market in the United States for the past twenty years, created and protected by those who fervently believe in it, things have hardly improved for large groups of people, and even fewer people are bound to profit from it in the future."[10] Rieger argues that "the contribution of theological and religious reflection to the further development of economics and the tremendous powers that it represents is . . . [in the service] of finding glimpses of an alternative reality. The best chances for this to happen

---

8. See Devinney et al., *Myth of the Ethical Consumer*.
9. Bulaong, "Explicitly Integrating Systemic/Institutional Thinking," 15–21.
10. Rieger, *No Rising Tide*, 15.

INTRODUCTION

are in places where the pressures of the economic and ecological status quo become unbearable and are therefore being challenged."[11]

Chapter 1 discusses the challenge of wicked problems, which are a way of framing structures of sin to help communities more concretely articulate and respond to the complexities of said structures. These are also opportunities for disruption, where we can explore how we might create alternative ways of doing business that are more directed towards the common good and challenge mainstream business and economics. Chapter 2 then talks about how Catholic social thought has responded to these structures of sin through particular principles and concepts that form the foundation of Catholic social thought. These principles are important and helpful guides for ethical disruption but also have limitations, given the work needed to challenge the status quo.

Given these limitations, Chapter 3 turns towards design thinking—one tool that can be used to concretely address wicked problems. It is a fruitful dialogue partner that can help operationalize Catholic social thought in crafting contextual solutions for organizations seeking to do good business. Chapter 4 then explores the dialogue points between Catholic social thought and design thinking, and the implications of this dialogue for moving forward. Lastly, Chapter 5 elaborates on the principles grounded in said dialogue that would help guide business practice and help businesses move towards becoming structures of grace.

Bringing design thinking and its understanding of wicked problems and how to respond to them with the vision of society and principles found in Catholic social thought can strengthen business ethicists' and practitioners' ability to describe and respond to destructive structural or systemic dynamics—what Catholic social thought calls structures of sin—that underlie unethical practices in business and organizational culture. This cross-disciplinary conversation also provides resources for transforming such unethical systems and dynamics by offering principles for structuring and evaluating improvements in the organization and practices comprising the business value chain, towards an ethical form of disruption that offers a more sustainable form of business geared towards the common good.

My work hopes to contribute to what Rieger calls "glimpses of an alternative reality," by considering ways to create structures in business to help people do the good more easily and habituate the virtues that business ethicists wish business practitioners to embrace. This will be done using

11. Rieger, *No Rising Tide*, 27.

Introduction

design thinking and wicked problems, a method that is familiar to business people, and concepts and principles from Catholic social thought.[12] Catholic social thought may not be as familiar to business people, but, in this book, this modern tradition of religious discourse can contribute to a guiding framework for moving business structures towards being more conducive for human and environmental flourishing.

---

12. Catholic social thought refers to a body of work that brings to bear the insights and convictions of the Christian faith to the current sociopolitical and economic context. This includes work that was written and developed by Church leadership, such as popes or bishops, or theologians who are not necessarily part of the hierarchy. This body of work applies insight taken from religious sources such as scripture and tradition to the current context. Catholic social teaching, on the other hand, refers to a specific set of magisterial documents written by the Church leadership. Catholic social thought includes Catholic social teaching as well as work from other theologians.

Catholic social thought can offer principles to live by and to apply to one's own context. Catholic social teaching does not offer detailed and specific policy proposals on various issues, though theologians and ethicists have applied the principles to specific cases and thus have offered suggestions of policies or projects that might dovetail with Catholic social thought.

CHAPTER 1

The Challenge of Wicked Problems in Business

WHAT EXACTLY IS CATHOLIC social thought seeking to disrupt in business? What opportunities are there for people to use Catholic social thought to develop the way business is done?

In order to clarify the kinds of situations and problems that are being addressed, we look at the concept of wicked problems. Wicked problems are the kinds of problem that design thinking is primarily concerned with, and businesses often find themselves facing. Businesses recognize that wicked problems have helped them understand the difficulties they face in their operations and as opportunities for disruption. To further clarify the issues and goods at stake and move forward with possible solutions, we can frame structures of sin in business as wicked problems. This chapter begins with a discussion of the structures of sin in Catholic social thought, then will move to the connection between wicked problems and structures of sin.

STRUCTURES OF SIN IN CATHOLIC SOCIAL THOUGHT AND THEOLOGY

Structures of sin and grace are an important part of Catholic social thought. When businesses are disrupted and move away from these structures, these disruptions become a major concern in the field of Catholic social thought. The question is, what are the structures of sin and how do these reflect the characteristics of wicked problems? "Structures of sin" is a category that tries to capture the experience and dynamics of systemic injustice in the world. The developing movement of liberation theology in the 1960s made the concept of "structures of sin" more prominent among Latin American theologians. Because of the growing recognition in Catholic social thought of the complexity of sin and evil in the world, the term began to find its way into magisterial documents such as *Justice in the World* in 1971.

"Structures of sin" denote systems and ways of being that violate and oppress human dignity and promote selfishness rather than solidarity. Silent acquiescence to oppressive acts and structures is also a part of this concept.[1] It destroys the vision that God has for creation and its flourishing, rupturing the relationships between God, human beings, and creation, and is therefore morally wrong.[2] Conversely, "structures of grace" are described as structures that enable flourishing of such interrelationships—precisely the opposite of structures of sin.

Christian theological anthropology ties the concepts of social sin and structures of sin in Catholic social teaching: human beings, as created by God, are radically social and relational, and therefore cannot be totally separated from the communities and contexts within which they live. People are not self-made; their values, ways of life, and ways of thinking are all affected by—though not solely determined by—the other people and their actions that make up the particular social context in which they are situated.[3]

This is also a sociological idea: people and the systems and structures created by human action interact with and are affected by each other. Sociologists Peter Berger and Thomas Luckmann would describe this dynamic of interaction and effect as a process of externalization, objectivation, and internalization: "society is a human product. Society is an objective reality. Man is a social product."[4]

In the process of externalization, human beings create and support values, patterns of behavior, languages, and institutions through creative activity. These patterns of behavior and institutions become an objective part of the social site. They have their own facticity and now confront and impinge their particular logic on human beings. This then leads to an internalization where human beings begin to be formed (or malformed) by the institutions and systems that exist. This is an important insight into

1. Whitehead and Whitehead, "Attending to the Experience of Injustice," 128–29.
2. Gutiérrez, *Theology of Liberation*.
3. See Fernandez, *Reimagining the Human*; Bowles and Gintis, *Cooperative Species*; Grenz, *Social God and the Relational Self*.
4. Berger and Luckmann, *Social Construction of Reality*, 61.

The Challenge of Wicked Problems in Business

how human beings interact with their contexts and to understand patterns of injustice and patterns of sin. This is also why, in recent years, Catholic theologians and ethicists as well as official Catholic social teaching have paid increased attention to these social and structural aspects of sin.

At this point, it's important to clear up a few of the terms used in this book. Structures of sin and grace are used as theological terms. We also need to distinguish these terms from other common terms such as "unethical structures," or "structures for solidarity" and "structures for the common good." These are terms used by business ethicists to refer to the structural issues in business that either help or hinder good business. Structures of evil and structures of grace, respectively, are not equivalent terms. The terms "unethical structures," "structures of solidarity," and "structures for the common good" still retain their value, however, especially in dialogue with non-Christian and non-religious business people.

Traditional business language is not unfamiliar with the idea of unethical structures. However, the identification of such is often reduced to legalistic language, whereby an unethical structure is simply one that does not comply with the law. When you keep this in mind, to be an ethical business may also be reduced to simply complying with the law. The term "unethical structures" does not fully capture the complexity of such formative structures, the injustice that such a structure can perpetuate legalistic understanding, that inculcates particular values in the persons who participate in them, affecting or violating relationships.

In the financial crisis of 2008, some regarded the lack of ethics merely as the lack of transparency and regulation. "If only there were stricter compliance with regulations, such unjust outcomes would have been avoided." With Catholic theology, we need a deeper look at such systems, and require investigating the deeper dynamics beyond adherence to regulations.

On the opposite end though, the language of "structures of solidarity" and "structures for the common good" has also entered the business milieu. These concepts may be helpful to signify a movement towards the well-being of people and creation, especially in a pluralistic setting. While structures of grace might emphasize the transcendent and undertaking towards the holy, the language of structures for the common good or solidarity could highlight the importance of the physical and spiritual well-being, as well as the relationships among people and the environment. However, similar to the concept of unethical structures, these concepts do not necessarily capture the formative aspect of such structures.

From a theological perspective, God and God's connection to these structures also come to question. It is something that is not as discussed when speaking only of unethical structures or structures of solidarity or for the common good. The terms sin and grace also imply questions on the connection between these structures with God and a person's faith commitment. This faith relationship may not necessarily be a point of agreement for mutual dialogue when Christian and non-Christian business people dialogue with each other, but it does remind Christians that there is something more at stake when Christians engage in the work of justice in the world of business.

Structures of Sin in Magisterial Documents

While the specific terminology of structures of sin and its related terms entered Catholic social thought only in the late 1960s and 70s with the interaction of liberation theology and post-Vatican II theology, earlier documents had already begun to describe the complicity of people in supporting dehumanizing patterns in society. Formulating the insight that social structures can also oppress people and promote individual acts of selfishness and evil has already been formulating as well. We now turn to discuss structures of sin in magisterial documents and their characteristics that reflect their similarities to wicked problems.

Rerum Novarum (1891)

Leo XIII, while focusing on working conditions and rejecting the commodification of human labor, critiques ideologies such as socialism and liberal capitalism and their dehumanizing systemic effects. Instead, he pushes for socioeconomic justice. As ethicist Bernard Brady points out, Leo XIII importantly presents that "poverty is not simply caused by bad luck or the laziness of people; it can be caused by the way economic systems are structured."[5]

Rerum Novarum ("On Capital and Labor") accuses individuals who advance unjust ideologies and structures. An example given was workers left to "the hardheartedness of employers and the greed of unchecked competition."[6] The pope focuses on the dynamic between worker and em-

---

5. Brady, *Essential Catholic Social Thought*, 70.
6. Leo XIII, *Rerum Novarum*, sec. 3.

ployee, their respective rights and duties to each other, and the roles of various institutions such as the government. This act acknowledges that the economic dynamics among these groups and institutions—expressed primarily through the actions of the powerful—can have negative effects on people, and requires a response from those in power to correct unjust practices and unfair working conditions.

Quadragesimo Anno (1931)

Quadragesimo Anno ("On Reconstruction of the Social Order") continues to elaborate on the themes present in *Rerum Novarum*. In the fourth paragraph, Pius XI acknowledges:

> Quite agreeable, of course, [is] this state of things to those who [think] their abundant riches are the result of inevitable economic laws and accordingly, as if it were for charity to veil the violation of justice which lawmakers not only tolerated but at times sanctioned, wanted the whole care of supporting the poor committed to charity alone.[7]

Although they did not use the term social sin, *Quadragesimo Anno* echoes Leo XIII that the dynamics of economic liberalism and monopoly capitalism coupled with the concentration of wealth—and consequently, power—in the hands of the few, as condoned by governments and businesses, had continued to degrade workers' lives.[8] Pius XI focuses on institutions when describing wicked problems, as well as the relationships between groups and individuals, which have both positive and negative effects on people. It was his recommendation that public institutions be reformed in order to make society conform to the "needs of the common good; that is, to the norm of social justice."[9] This would be achieved, he argues, by a return to Christian moderation and gospel values.[10]

---

7. Pius XI, *Quadragesimo Anno*, sec. 4.
8. Pius XI, *Quadragesimo Anno*, secs. 105–9.
9. Pius XI, *Quadragesimo Anno*, sec. 110.
10. Pius XI, *Quadragesimo Anno*, secs. 136–37.

Mater et Magistra (1961)

In *Mater et Magistra* ("On Christianity and Social Progress"), John XXIII emphasizes the "increase in social relationships . . . scientific and technical progress, greater productive efficiency, and a higher standard of living are among the many present-day factors which would have seem to have contributed to this trend."[11] *Mater et Magistra* points out both the advantages and disadvantages of this process of "socialization":

> Clearly, this sort of development in social relationships brings many advantages in its train. It makes it possible for the individual to exercise many of his personal rights, especially those which we call economic and social. . . . At the same time, however, this multiplication and daily extension of forms of association brings with it a multiplicity of restrictive laws and regulations in many departments of human life. . . . The means often used, the methods followed, the atmosphere created, all conspire to make it difficult for a person to think independently of outside influences, to act on his own initiative, exercise his responsibility and express and fulfil his own personality.[12]

On one hand, the increasing interrelationship allows for a synergy in helping people exercise their rights and fulfill their needs. However, this same synergy and aggregation of behavior and connections can also amplify the negative effects of what would have otherwise been minute consequences of very localized actions, which we may not be aware of, as wicked problems warn. For example, as associations and corporations grow in number and scope, they are able to create more affordable products and services for the people. Unfortunately, they often generate high levels of pollution and waste that contribute to the current environmental crisis. Social sin is frequently described in similar ways today. The actions of several people create a bigger effect than the mere aggregation of their individual work—the whole becomes greater than the sum of its parts.

Foundational to understanding structures of sin is the notion of the common good, which *Mater et Magistra* defines as "all those social conditions which favor the full development of human personality."[13] John XXIII recognizes that the presence (or absence) of such social conditions or structures has an important effect on human flourishing. He implies

---

11. John XXIII, *Mater et Magistra*, sec. 59.
12. John XXIII, *Mater et Magistra*, secs. 61–62.
13. John XXIII, *Mater et Magistra*, sec. 65.

that creating and perpetuating structures that favor human flourishing is a Christian and civic duty. An important part of this civic duty also includes maintaining the balance between the freedom of individuals and the activity of the state.

Pacem in Terris (1963) and Gaudium et Spes (1965)

Pacem in Terris ("On Establishing Universal Peace in Truth, Justice, Charity, and Liberty") emphasizes that a well-ordered society is, by nature, moral, grounded in truth and guided by social justice. Its moral relationships among people in a good society can be described in terms of rights and duties. Acknowledging these rights and duties can help people understand and enact justice and charity. However, *Pacem in Terris* also points out that many present social structures are inadequate in promoting the common good. These structures are not necessarily called sinful in the document; however, John XXIII interrogates these structures.

In articulating its suggestions for ways to create the necessary conditions for human development, *Pacem in Terris* does not simply recommend individual actions or a return to Christian values. Instead, it focuses on structural issues, the ways public authority should be organized, and the ways different nation states should relate to each other through consent and not force.[14] Similar to super wicked problems, it also notes the importance of a regulating body or central authority that can facilitate cooperation and harness the efforts and work of various individuals, groups, and nations towards the good.

In *Gaudium et Spes* ("On the Church in the Modern World"), the Second Vatican Council bishops reiterate the theme of human dignity present in previous documents to elaborate on the need to work towards being free from ignorance. *Gaudium et Spes* also emphasizes that once economic structures are created, they should remain under the control of human persons, rather than being allowed to freely take their course.[15] This is opposed to the defenders of "free markets" who argue that as long as the economic system is allowed to follow its due course, it would bring good to all. Instead, *Gaudium et Spes* emphasizes that these systems are not simply morally neutral or good, nor are they guaranteed to bring about the good all the time.

14. John XXIII, *Pacem in Terris*, secs. 135–38, 147–67.
15. Second Vatican Council, *Gaudium et Spes*, sec. 65.

While the inadequacy of humanly constructed systems and structures has been acknowledged before, both these documents introduce explicitly structural recommendations, particularly at the political level, as well as exhortations to individual action. One also detects an implicit acknowledgement that systems are neither morally neutral nor necessarily good, and that their moral status depends on what human beings make them to be.[16]

Populorum Progressio (1967)

In the wake of decolonization and growing concerns about socioeconomic development in the global south after the 1960s, the idea that structures prevented poorer countries from attaining authentic human development arose with increasing frequency in official Catholic social teaching. In *Populorum Progressio* ("On the Development of Peoples"), Paul VI outlines standards for judging whether particular changes in society are in line with authentic human development. He also acknowledges that society has inherited both good and bad structures and behavior from past generations and current generations have benefited from or are hindered by this past work. Paul VI in *Populorum Progressio* wishes to make clear that to eliminate injustice and create the conditions for authentic human development and flourishing, charity is not enough and that structural changes must be enacted:

> But these efforts, as well as public and private allocations of gifts, loans, and investments, are not enough. It is not just a question of eliminating hunger and reducing poverty. It is not just a question of fighting wretched conditions, though this is an urgent and necessary task. It involves building a human community where men can live truly human lives, free from discrimination on account of race, religion, or nationality, free from servitude to other men or to natural forces which they cannot yet control satisfactorily. It involves building a human community where liberty is not an idle word, where the needy Lazarus can sit down with the rich man at the same banquet table.[17]

Building the community requires more than just charity or gifts. It requires creating systems that allow for people to thrive and not just survive.

---

16. See Baum, *Religion and Alienation*.
17. Paul VI, *Populorum Progressio*, sec. 47.

Furthermore, in line with the previous popes' endorsement of the principle of subsidiarity, Paul VI emphasizes that the work needed to accomplish structural changes cannot simply come from the top public authorities. These authorities still need to instigate change, as expressed in *Rerum Novarum*; however, *Populorum Progressio* insists that the people themselves need to take active part in civic life and not just passively rely on the state.[18] While structures of sin or grace are not explicitly mentioned, the document points to such concepts in describing a way forward for the human community. As envisioned by *Populorum Progressio*, the institutional or cultural changes that move society away from the various "-isms" such as sexism, racism, or classicism, should be undertaken through negotiation and consensus, rather than conflict and violent revolution.

Justice in the World (1971)

The World Synod of Catholic Bishops' 1971 document acknowledges what today would be understood as structures of sin. The bishops have "been able to perceive the serious injustices which are building around the human world a network of domination, oppression and abuses ... which keep the greater part of humanity from sharing in the building up and enjoyment of a more just and more loving world."[19] Unjust systems and structures have kept many people oppressed, with an early critique of what will later on be called trickle-down economics:

> In the last twenty-five years, a hope has spread through the human race that economic growth would bring about such a quantity of goods that it would be possible to feed the hungry at least with the crumbs falling from the table, but this has proved a vain hope in underdeveloped areas and in pockets of poverty in wealthier areas, because of the rapid growth of population and of the labor force, because of rural stagnation and the lack of agrarian reform, and because of the massive migratory flow to the cities, where the industries, even though endowed with huge sums of money, nevertheless provide so few jobs that not infrequently one worker in four is left unemployed.[20]

---

18. Paul VI, *Populorum Progressio*, sec. 13.
19. World Synod of Catholic Bishops, *Justice in the World*, sec. 3.
20. World Synod of Catholic Bishops, *Justice in the World*, sec. 10.

Justice in the World reiterates the need for liberation from oppressive situations and emphasizes that action on behalf of justice is a constitutive dimension of the preaching of the Gospel. According to the bishops, "the bringing about of justice depends more and more on the determined will for development" by the developing nations.[21] They acknowledge that unjust social structures are a serious obstacle to genuine conversion and the doing of the good. Action on behalf of justice also requires both diagnosis and strategizing on a global and interrelated scale. Highlighting the accountability of those in power and responsible dovetails with the emphasis in wicked problems that the designers or problem solvers have "no right to be wrong," as Rittel put it.

Reconciliatio et Paenitentia (1984)

Reconciliatio et Paenitentia ("On Reconciliation and Penance"), an apostolic exhortation issued by John Paul II where he explains in detail his understanding of social sin, is not often included in the literature of Catholic social teaching, but the document contains by far the most extensive treatment of the concept of social sin in magisterial documents to date. It is also one of the first documents to include the term, drawn from the Latin American bishops' conferences and Latin American theologians' work.[22]

John Paul II explicitly roots social and structures sin in individual acts that always have social repercussions.[23] He rejects the idea that structures can themselves be sinful, and thus always traces responsibility for oppressive structures to the action of particular human beings, rooted in greed and idolatry. To speak of social sin acknowledges that: (1) "by virtue of human solidarity . . . each individual's sin in some way affects others"; (2) "some sins . . . are an offense against God because they are offenses against one's neighbor"; and (3) "relationships [between various human communities] are not always in accordance with the plan of God, for there to be justice in the world and freedom and peace between individuals, groups, and peoples."[24] The pope knows the difficulty of attributing moral responsibility to individual people in certain situations where the causes and effects are complex and sometimes unclear. Nevertheless, he argues that those

---

21. World Synod of Catholic Bishops, *Justice in the World*, sec. 13.
22. John Paul II, *Reconciliatio et Paenitentia*; John Paul II, *Sollicitudo Rei Socialis*.
23. John Paul II, *Reconciliatio et Paenitentia*, sec. 16.
24. John Paul II, *Reconciliatio et Paenitentia*, sec. 16.

who describe social situations as sinful are speaking analogously, and that it should not lead to a complacency in understanding how individual acts support and perpetuate these situations. John Paul II stresses this point, stating significantly, that:

> Whenever the church speaks of situations of sin or when she condemns as structures of sins certain situations or the collective behavior of certain social groups, big or small, or even of whole nations and blocs of nations, she knows and she proclaims that such cases of structures of sin are the result of the accumulation and concentration of many personal sins. It is a case of the very personal sins of those who cause or support evil or who exploit it; of those who are in a position to avoid, eliminate or at least limit certain social evils but who fail to do so out of laziness, fear or the conspiracy of silence, through secret complicity or indifference; of those who take refuge in the supposed impossibility of changing the world and also of those who sidestep the effort and sacrifice required, producing specious reasons of higher order. The real responsibility, then, lies with individuals. A situation—or likewise an institution, a structure, society itself—is not in itself the subject of moral acts. Hence a situation cannot in itself be good or bad.[25]

John Paul II rejects the notion that blame can be placed on "some vague entity or anonymous collectivity such as the situation, the system, society, structures or institutions."[26] Because situations, systems, or structures lack the moral agency to "choose" to harm or do good, they cannot therefore be called sinful, as sin is always tied to some form of willful choosing. Hence, John Paul II continually returns to the individuals whose choices create or perpetuate such contexts as the sinful agents.

Sollicitudo Rei Socialis (1987)

Sollicitudo Rei Socialis, issued on the twentieth anniversary of *Populorum Progressio*, speaks explicitly of "structures of sin," underscoring that "the principal obstacle to be overcome on the way to authentic liberation is sin and the structures produced by sin as it multiplies and spreads."[27] John Paul

---

25. John Paul II, *Reconciliatio et Paenitentia*, sec. 16; John Paul II, *Sollicitudo Rei Socialis*, sec. 36.

26. John Paul II, *Reconciliatio et Paenitentia*, sec. 16.

27. John Paul II, *Sollicitudo Rei Socialis*, sec. 46.

II strongly calls for the reformation of unjust structures that impede authentic human development, in both the east and the west:

> It is important to note therefore that a world which is divided into blocs, sustained by rigid ideologies, and in which instead of interdependence and solidarity different forms of imperialism hold sway, can only be a world subject to structures of sin. The sum total of the negative factors working against a true awareness of the universal common good, and the need to further it, gives the impression of creating, in persons and institutions, an obstacle which is difficult to overcome.[28]

Similar to wicked problems, *Sollicitudo Rei Socialis* outlines the various ills that are symptomatic of the problem of stunted development, and how these ills are interconnected. The pope roots these sinful structures in two particular vices: an "all-consuming desire for profit" and a "thirst for power . . . at any price." Individuals and groups can exhibit such attitudes. "If certain forms of modern 'imperialism' were considered in the light of these moral criteria, hidden behind certain decisions, apparently inspired only by economics or politics, are real forms of idolatry: of money, ideology, class, technology."[29] Thus, "it is a question of moral evil, the fruit of many sins which lead to 'structures of sin.'"[30] John Paul II then refers extensively to *Reconciliatio et Paenitentia*, stating that:

> If the present situation can be attributed to difficulties of various kinds, it is not out of place to speak of "structures of sin," which, as I stated in my Apostolic Exhortation *Reconciliatio et Paenitentia*, are rooted in personal sin, and thus always linked to the concrete acts of individuals who introduce these structures, consolidate them and make them difficult to remove. And thus they grow stronger, spread, and become the source of other sins, and so influence people's behavior.[31]

John Paul II moves the conversation on social sin and structures of sin forward by connecting how structures of sin affect people's behavior, without discounting individual responsibility.

---

28. John Paul II, *Sollicitudo Rei Socialis*, sec. 36.
29. John Paul II, *Sollicitudo Rei Socialis*, sec. 37.
30. John Paul II, *Sollicitudo Rei Socialis*, sec. 37.
31. John Paul II, *Sollicitudo Rei Socialis*, sec. 36.

Centesimus Annus (1991)

In this 1991 document, John Paul II critiques socialism, offering a cautious and nuanced understanding of what forms of capitalism would support the common good. *Centesimus Annus* ("On the Hundredth Anniversary of Rerum Novarum") is concerned with social structures, particularly political and economic and on a global scale, in response to the fall of communism. Like *Sollicitudo Rei Socialis*, it explicitly uses the language of social structures and "structures of sin" in describing how human beings interact within their surrounding contexts:

> Man receives from God his essential dignity and with it the capacity to transcend every social order so as to move towards truth and goodness. But he is also conditioned by the social structure in which he lives, by the education he has received and by his environment. These elements can either help or hinder his living in accordance with the truth. The decisions which create a human environment can give rise to specific structures of sin which impede the full realization of those who are in any way oppressed by them. To destroy such structures and replace them with more authentic forms of living in community is a task which demands courage and patience.[32]

The definition of structures of sin is taken directly from *Reconciliatio et Paenitentia*. Significantly, *Centesimus Annus* also emphasizes the need for positive structures that reinforce participation and shared responsibility rather than the structures of concentrated power.[33]

Caritas in Veritate (2009)

Writing on the heels of the 2008 global financial crisis, Benedict XVI critiques the practice of speculative finance and other economic activities that contributed to the crisis. He also comments on the various dynamics and trends that pervade the contemporary socioeconomic and political situation while highlighting the interconnected of the various issues of the time. In *Caritas in Veritate* ("On Integral Human Development In Charity and Truth"), Benedict XVI argues that "to take a stand for the common good is on the one hand to be solicitous for, and on the other hand to avail oneself

---

32. John Paul II, *Centesimus Annus*, sec. 38.
33. John Paul II, *Centesimus Annus*, secs. 43–46.

of, that complex of institutions that give structure to the life of society, juridically, civilly, politically and culturally, making it the polis, or 'city.'"[34] The socioeconomic and political spheres are neither ethically neutral nor opposed to human beings, and thus, the structures that are needed for the common good ought to be structured in an ethical manner.[35]

Benedict XVI follows his predecessor in emphasizing individual and personal responsibility. He further argues that "integral human development presupposes the responsible freedom of the individual and of peoples: no structure can guarantee this development over and above human responsibility."[36] He observes that "Paul VI had a keen sense of the importance of economic structures and institutions, but he had an equally clear sense of their nature as instruments of human freedom. Only when it is free can development be integrally human; only in a climate of responsible freedom can it grow in a satisfactory manner."[37] In order to honor the importance of freedom in integral human development, *Caritas in Veritate* endorses structures that are open to gratuitousness and communion, rooted in actions and a deeper logic that go beyond power struggles or commodified exchange.

Evangelii Gaudium (2013), *Laudato Si'* (2015) and *Laudato Deum* (2023)

Francis, for his part, even more strongly critiques contemporary economic and social structures, particularly those that have excluded others, and how they all relate to each other as one complex problem. In his statements on trickle-down economics cited above, this pope rejects the assumption that economics is morally neutral, or that it will automatically bring about greater justice, if only it is left to its own devices. He roots the support of trickle-down economics in an idolatry of the market and critiques the idea of social systems being served and worshipped, rather than being in the service of human beings—often to the detriment of the poor.[38] The trickle-down system "is evil crystallized in unjust social structures, which cannot be the basis of hope for a better future . . . since the conditions

---

34. Benedict XVI, *Caritas in Veritate*, sec. 7.
35. Benedict XVI, *Caritas in Veritate*, sec. 36.
36. Benedict XVI, *Caritas in Veritate*, sec. 17.
37. Benedict XVI, *Caritas in Veritate*, sec. 17.
38. Francis, *Evangelii Gaudium*, secs. 54–59.

for a sustainable and peaceful development have not yet been adequately articulated and realized."[39]

In his treatment of integral ecology, Francis acknowledges oppressive systems to be sinful, especially when they produce not only social injustice but also environmental injustice and imbalances in power. In appreciating the intrinsic and complex links between social crises and the environmental crisis, Francis points to one massive and complex system that is interconnected, rather than individual problems and people in compartmentalized situations:

> Given the scale of change, it is no longer possible to find a specific, discrete answer for each part of the problem. We are faced not with two separate crises, one environmental and the other social, but rather with one complex crisis which is both social and environmental. Strategies for a solution demand an integrated approach to combating poverty, restoring dignity to the excluded, and at the same time protecting nature.[40]

He recognizes Christianity's complicity in the problem and points to the ways various social and religious institutions are connected together in the web of crises and ruptured relationships. Francis identifies the "technocratic paradigm," a way of seeing the world which assumes that scientific and technological progress automatically improves and develops human life. The paradigm also reflects a power and privilege imbalance between those who have access to such technological progress and those who have not, plus the fact that this access has not necessarily been linked with more ethical awareness and responsibility.[41]

Francis continues his discussion of the technocratic paradigm in *Laudato Deum* ("On the Climate Crisis"), particularly in how the technocratic paradigm contributes to the dominance of particular groups of people over others; The technocratic paradigm includes how facts and information related to the climate crisis are distorted and derided, creating a culture of disinformation.[42] Francis also discusses the use of power in the technocratic paradigm, and how "not every increase in power represents progress for humanity"; thus, there is a need to rethink what power means, its limits,

---

39. Francis, *Evangelii Gaudium*, sec. 59.

40. Francis, *Laudato Si'*, sec. 139.

41. Zenner, "Commentary on *Laudato Si'*," locs. 17565–72, in Himes, *Modern Catholic Social Teaching*.

42. Francis, *Laudate Deum*, secs. 20–23, 29.

and the "need for lucidity and honesty in order to recognize in time that our power and the progress we are producing are turning against us."[43]

In a society ruled by the technocratic paradigm, people are easily overwhelmed by contemporary structures of power and injustice.[44] The imbalance of power fostered by this paradigm has, according to Francis, paralyzed human beings into inaction, fatalism, and complicity, as people may think that there is nothing they can do, and that any action on their part would not make a difference.

Final Document of the Amazon Synod (2019), *Querida Amazonia* (2020), and *Fratelli Tutti* (2020)

The two documents of the Amazon Synod of Bishops continue the rejection of "situations of sin, structures of death, violence, and injustice."[45] The *Final Document of the Amazon Synod*, issued by the bishops of the region, reiterates the ecological sin Francis describes in *Laudato Si'* ("On Care for Our Common Home") together with the ecological crises' negative effects on the most vulnerable when describing the "cry of the earth and the cry of the poor."[46] Both identify complex problems of economic migration and climate crisis in the region, which are exacerbated by the problematic economic, political, and social structures, and further highlights the relationships among various social issues, including how they aggravate the plight of marginalized groups in the region. The points raised concerning social structures are not only applicable to the region; there is also the connection to the condition of the region to the wider global situation, highlighting how the interaction of the local and global affect people, whether positively or negatively.

Fratelli Tutti ("On Fraternity and Social Friendship") continues Francis's broad concern for economic structures that exploit and harm rather than help people flourish.[47] The document warns not only against

---

43. Francis, *Laudate Deum*, secs. 24, 28.

44. Francis, *Laudato Si'*, sec. 53.

45. Synod of Bishops for the Pan-Amazon, *Final Document of the Amazon Synod*, sec. 48.

46. Synod of Bishops for the Pan-Amazon, *Final Document of the Amazon Synod*, secs. 10–14.

47. See Heyer, *Walls in the Heart*, 26–28. Heyer deals with Francis's broad understanding of social sin in *Fratelli Tutti* and how he develops this understanding of social sin in relation to emerging theologies.

structures that deny human rights, but also warns against structures that exclude other people and limit one's sense of community or neighbor.[48] These structures make it more difficult to work together for the common good: "in some parts of our world, individuals or peoples are prevented from developing their potential and beauty by poverty or other structural limitations. In the end, this will impoverish us all."[49]

Structures of Sin in Select Theologians' Work

Contemporary theologians have, in dialogue with other disciplines like sociology, elaborated the reflection on structures of sin and how they manifest themselves in human institutions, particularly in a more globalized community. Scholars have also sought to describe the ways structures of sin have systemically kept certain groups of people from achieving justice and human flourishing.[50]

It was in the Latin American context that theological treatments of structural sin really began to be fleshed out in the 1960s and 1970s. Latin American liberation theologians, such as Gustavo Gutiérrez, were pioneers in developing the concept of structures of sin. In his groundbreaking 1972 work, *A Theology of Liberation*, Gutiérrez remarks:

> Sin—a breach of friendship with God and others—is according to the Bible the ultimate cause of poverty, injustice, and the oppression in which the persons lives. In describing sin as the ultimate cause, we do not in any way negate the structural reasons and the objective determinants leading to these situations. It does, however, emphasize the fact that things do not happen by chance and that behind an unjust structure there is a persona or collective will responsible.[51]

Drawing from the Latin American Bishops' Conference in Medellín, Colombia in 1968, Gutiérrez points out that unjust political and economic systems in Latin America did not happen by chance or by accident. Rather, the injustice was perpetuated through institutions that amplified the sinfulness of certain human agents.[52]

48. Francis, *Fratelli Tutti*, sec. 102.
49. Francis, *Fratelli Tutti*, sec. 137.
50. Kelly, "Nature and Operation of Structural Sin."
51. Gutiérrez, *Theology of Liberation*, 24.
52. Gutiérrez, *Theology of Liberation*, 102.

Other terms for structures of sin, such as "sin-solidarity," have also been proposed, as with the work of Gregory Baum and Mark O'Keefe. Baum describes four levels to social sin. The first level involves concrete injustices and dehumanizing patterns and trends found in social systems and institutions. The second level goes deeper, pointing to the different cultural and religious symbols assumed in society that underlie and reinforce the first level. The third level is what Baum identifies as a "false consciousness" or skewed worldview that assures people that the status quo of society, with its symbols, assumptions, and ethics are all morally right. Lastly, the fourth level of social sin is the collective action and work done based on the false worldview of the third level, including activities that further buttress the injustice of the systems that are already in place.[53]

O'Keefe, on the other hand, surveys the various terms used by theologians over time. He highlights their theological and sociological explanations of structures of sin, together with the meaning of conversion in light of their understanding of structures of sin. O'Keefe also emphasizes that "inasmuch as sin is *sin* and structures are built up by human choice and cooperation—sin can (theoretically at least) be traced, however tenuously or remotely, to some event or form of personal choosing. Once the choice is made, its effects then take on a history of their own."[54]

It can be difficult to identify the precise roots of such injustice, similar to wicked problems and their symptoms. Nevertheless, such injustices do occur, regardless of origin. Although it is often only noticed in hindsight, these injustices are perpetuated through human action, whether evil is consciously intended or not.[55] O'Keefe adds that in general, structures of sin involve a certain blindness or ignorance to the injustice of the situation one is enmeshed in; however, he insists, the excuse of ignorance should not be so quickly used.[56] O'Keefe also quotes various theologians saying that not only do structures of sin create and perpetuate injustice, they also encourage further personal sin by creating situations that make moral and ethical decision-making difficult. These situations that make doing the good more difficult also include situations that require compromise, and situations where there is no other recourse but to acknowledge that in the meantime, at least, evil cannot be avoided in the decision-making.

---

53. Baum, *Religion and Alienation*, 200–203.
54. O'Keefe, *What Are They Saying about Social Sin?*, 60.
55. O'Keefe, *What Are They Saying about Social Sin?*, 60–61.
56. O'Keefe, *What Are They Saying about Social Sin?*, 69–70.

The Challenge of Wicked Problems in Business

Theological ethicist Bryan Massingale, for example, describes a culture of indifference that has legitimized the "neglect for the poor . . . found in otherwise well-intentioned individuals." This has been caused by systemic issues of consumerism and racism, as well as a tendency to see poverty as solely a personal responsibility and not affected by social institutions or structures.[57] Theological ethicist Cristina Traina's definition of structures of sin also describes the situations that make moral decision making difficult with the unequal distribution of risks and benefits that arise out of these difficult situations. For Traina, "structural evil is the comprehensive complex of interdependent, overlapping systems that, by distributing risks, benefits, and harms unequally, generates an oversupply of violence, insecurity, and disadvantage for some and relative immunity from them for others."[58] This unjust distribution of risks and benefits is important to consider especially in business ethics, where managing risks has become even more crucial in the age of climate change and rapidly changing technology, social trends, and movements.

In referring to the phenomena mentioned above, theologian Bernard Lonergan describes the systemic blindness (*scotosis*) that people exhibit, in the form of biases, that arise from failure to reflect on and engage in ethical questioning of one's experiences and moral situations, in the corresponding processes of ongoing self-correction. Such biases, which can arise unconsciously, block the ability to form insights. When these accumulate over time, they produce what Lonergan calls long-term cycles of decline.[59] In these situations, general bias (lack of concern for long-term consequences), and group bias (discrimination against particular groups of people), spiral downwards into cycles of decline that encompass individuals, communities, and the environment. And, if the community continues to avoid self-correction, this can lead to their destruction.[60] Such cycles of decline are manifested in longer historical patterns of relations in social structures that perpetuate habitual injustice and the complicity of individuals. These structures allow people to "evad[e] or refus[e] a wider possibility to correct, to transform, or to rebuild patterns of social living."[61]

---

57. Massingale, "Scandal of Poverty," 62.
58. Traina, "This Is the Year," 4–5.
59. Lonergan, *Insight*, 242–57.
60. Lonergan, *Insight*, 218–32.
61. Melchin, *Living with Other People*, 45. See Lonergan, *Insight*, ch. 7.

In addition, cycles of decline can "transform [something evil that] was once a difficult action into effortless routine ... [and] as [these evil attitudes and actions] pass into the pattern of our living, they are taken up as tools for solving new problems or for developing new capacities and skills. So, too, they become justified and rationalized within an overall moral logic."[62] All of this need not be purposefully planned since the linked patterns of behavior that make up social structures "can emerge spontaneously to yield structures that achieve what none could achieve alone."[63] Significantly, such structures can actively work towards evil, depending on the human agency that is connected to cycles of decline. Canadian theologian Kenneth Melchin emphasizes that "as long as the emergent structures are not acknowledged, analyzed, and evaluated, their horrific impacts on marginalized groups can continue unchecked without anyone deliberately intending harm."[64]

Other theologians have also clarified the distinction between "structures of sin" and "social sin." These terms are at times used interchangeably in magisterial documents. In *Reconciliatio et Paenitentia*, John Paul II uses the term "social sin," but would later use "structures of sin" in *Sollicitudo Rei Socialis*, even as he cites his previous exhortation.[65] For Catholic ethicist Conor Kelly, structures of sin must be seen as a "species of a larger genus of social sin, which refers more broadly to all types of social influences that induce individuals to sin."[66]

There are also other theologians who have attempted to use different terms altogether. Daniel Daly, for example, cites that in light of post-Vatican II theological ethics, "structures of virtue" and "structures of vice" may more accurately capture the ways in which people relate with social structures and vice-versa. The language of structures of virtue and vice signals not only the ways in which particular systems do or don't promote the common good by influencing human actions, but also whether or not they shape a person's moral character towards moral excellence (virtue) or the opposite (vice).[67] He stresses that structures of vice "contain social rela-

---

62. Melchin, *Living with Other People*, 92. See Lonergan, *Insight*, ch. 7.
63. Melchin, *Living with Other People*, 94–95. See Lonergan, *Insight*, ch. 7.
64. Melchin, *Living with Other People*, 94–95. See Lonergan, *Insight*, ch. 7.
65. See *Reconciliatio et Paenitentia*, sec. 16, compared to *Sollicitudo Rei Socialis* sec. 36–38.
66. Kelly, "Nature and Operation of Structural Sin," 294.
67. Daly, "Structures of Virtue and Vice," 341–57.

tions that enable and facilitate the acquisition of vicious traits by those who participate in the structure. Vicious structures include positions in which persons are constrained in their ability to recognize and promote the dignity of others, especially the poor and marginalized."[68] The formative aspect of structures is an important characteristic of structures of sin and grace. In this regard, infusing design thinking into awareness of structure can help people do the good more readily as part of their habit.

STRUCTURES OF SIN IN BUSINESS ETHICS

Some theologians have begun drawing on the work on structures of sin to describe what is happening in business and economics. They continue the discussion on how even those who may seem innocent of any form of unethical business practice may still be complicit in systems that, although they do greater good, also cause greater harm. Two Catholic scholars working in this area are Dominican priest and economist Albino Barrera and theological ethicist Daniel Finn.

Barrera and Finn employ the language of structures of sin to present new ways of thinking about how people are complicit in and responsible for the injustice that social and economic structures create. Both scholars emphasize that the relationship between human agency and injustice can be complicated and muddled in these structures. Sometimes, it is difficult to draw a straight line between a human action as cause and injustice as effect. For Barrera, the tools and methods that Christian ethicists tend to use to discuss complicity in injustice and evil are inadequate to the task of describing or accounting for economic complicity. Economic complicity is defined as a situation where one individual participating in the economic market may not seem to do much harm, but multiplied to many individuals, the negative effect on communities who are not directly connected to the individual market actors becomes apparent.

Two tools often used by Christian ethicists are the principle of cooperation with evil, which deals with complicity by parsing out the degrees of responsibility, and the principle of double effect, which deals with complicity by providing specific criteria for evaluating whether a person can legitimately choose to do a seemingly wrong or evil action.[69]

---

68. Daly, *Structures of Virtue and Vice*, 169.

69. See McIntyre, "Doctrine of Double Effect"; Capps, "Formal and Material Cooperation with Evil," 681–98.

According to Barrera, both these principles are inadequate for addressing economic complicity. For one thing, they do not have any theory of causality. Moreover, it is difficult to weigh positive and harmful outcomes against each other, and it is difficult to identify the criteria for doing so. A commonly cited example is the wicked problem of sweatshop labor, where businesses source their products from factories which pay below minimum wage and have hazardous working conditions so consumers can buy cheap garments. While one individual buying from such a business may not do much harm, many people supporting such businesses, because they themselves cannot afford any better, would be indirectly supporting a harmful situation of worker exploitation. The impact of one individual supporting (or refusing to support) such a business that relies on sweatshop labor is not much, but many individuals when aggregated can create lasting effects, both good and bad.

Barrera further points out that the two principles are very individualistic in their understanding of complicity. They focus only on justifying particular actions and not the relationships of these actions with each other, their outcomes, and their agents. Such an individualistic approach will not work in the market, because the market is a structure of a complex web of interrelationships and agents, both individual and groups, that can do great harm (operating as a structure of sin) or good (operating as a structure of grace). Barrera draws on tort jurisprudence and Aristotelean-Thomistic philosophy in order to build his case for a person's moral obligation to take responsibility for harms both directly and indirectly caused. They need to take into account power and moral ambiguities in the face of economic markets that are further complicated by advancing technology and closer connections through globalization.

Catholic economist and ethicist Daniel Finn, on the other hand, proposes a framework to analyze market economies by identifying four important elements that comprise the moral ecology of any market economy. All of these need to be considered when making any ethical claims about said economies. The first is the "fences" that need to be placed within and around the economy to ensure that abuses are not committed. The second is the provision of essential goods and services. The third is the morality of individuals and groups of people. And the last is the presence of civil society.

Finn draws from Barrera in describing the moral complicity of a person when participating in the current market economy and business systems where one's actions may not seem to directly harm others. He also points out the coercive powers of the market and pricing structures contained therein.[70] In the current economic market, it is easy to think that the individual is free of responsibility for any moral harm, as the effect of one person is not obvious. Finn, however, links individual action with the moral harms inflicted in economic markets by identifying when economic compulsion has occurred (i.e., when the pricing structure of the market imposes costs on people whose well-being is threatened through forced participation in the said market). Finn argues that in cases of economic compulsion, "consumers as market participants, even at a great distance from the last link in the chain where the compulsion occurs, are morally responsible for the harm caused."[71]

WICKED PROBLEMS

Structures of sin, on their own, can be overwhelming as a category. The interrelated "-isms" that form structures of sin such as racism, classism, and sexism, can seem daunting and a problem that cannot be addressed.

    The concept of wicked problems is a helpful concept here. Wicked problems are complex problems that are notoriously difficult to solve, with a particular set of characteristics that make it wicked. In contrast, "tame" problems are problems that are straightforward and solved through more traditional analytical tools. While one can use design thinking for these tame problems, it would not be particularly useful nor efficient to do so. Wicked problems are called wicked because they are multi-causal and multi-factorial. They are notoriously difficult to address and solve, and any attempt to solve them is likely to yield unintended consequences.[72] Design thinking practitioners understand that human persons are complex beings with various motivations, thoughts, and circumstances, all of which can affect how a wicked problem is understood and how it can be solved. Traditional linear analytical tools are simply not adequate to solve these problems.

    The concept of wicked problems was developed in the late 1960s by a design theorist, Horst Rittel. He argued for using the label to describe a "class of social system problems which are ill-formulated, with

---

70. Finn, *Distant Markets*, 243–60.
71. Finn, *Distant Markets*, 257–58.
72. Rittel and Webber, "Dilemmas in a General Theory of Planning," 160.

confusing information, with many clients and decision makers with conflicting values, and where the ramifications in the whole system are thoroughly confusing."[73] To further flesh out the concept, Rittel identifies ten features of a wicked problem:[74]

1. There is no definitive formulation of a wicked problem.

Rittel describes wicked problems as indeterminate, but it does not mean that they are totally undetermined. Indeterminate in this case means that there are no completely definitive conditions or no single exhaustive explanation. Indeterminate can also refer to the locus of the problem, which is not always clear or identifiable. These indeterminacies make it difficult to decide how to frame or formulate the problem.

2. Wicked problems have no "stopping rule."

In traditional "tame" problems, we typically know when goals have been accomplished (e.g., when a math problem is solved). Wicked problems, however, have no such criteria for closure. "The process of solving the [wicked] problem is identical with the process of understanding its nature ... [and] because there are no criteria for sufficient understanding and because there are no ends to the causal chains that link interacting open systems, the would-be planner can always try to do better."[75] Given this, "the planner terminates work on a wicked problem, not for reasons inherent in the 'logic' of the problem. He stops for considerations that are external to the problem: he runs out of time, or money, or patience."[76]

3. Solutions to wicked problems are not true-or-false but rather good-or-bad.

Tame problems have clear criteria but for wicked problems, it is not the same. The many different causes, factors, stakeholders, and formulations of the problem make identifying correct solutions more complicated. There are a number of stakeholders who are affected by and who would judge the solutions. Each group will have their own judgements that accord to their own interests, perspectives, and values. Thus, solutions are seen

---

73. Churchman, "Guest Editorial," 141.
74. Rittel and Webber, "Dilemmas in a General Theory of Planning."
75. Rittel and Webber, "Dilemmas in a General Theory of Planning," 162.
76. Rittel and Webber, "Dilemmas in a General Theory of Planning," 162.

as either "good" that they help improve the situation for stakeholders, or "bad" that they worsen the situation for stakeholders.

4. There is no immediate test of a solution to a wicked problem.

Once a tame problem is solved that ends the problem. When it comes to wicked problems, however, once someone implements a possible solution, that solution will create changes. These changes will inevitably have new consequences within the systems, potentially over an unbounded period of time. The full consequences of the changes will only become known after the solution has been generated, and often only over a lengthy period of time.

5. Every solution to a wicked problem is a "one-shot operation." Since there is no opportunity to learn by trial-and-error, every attempt counts significantly but remains experimental.

It is difficult to ascertain all the repercussions of solutions to wicked problems, as well as their longevity and permanence. Therefore, every iteration or solution is consequential. The consequences of each solution are not easily undone—lives would have been influenced greatly, and vast resources would have been spent. Each attempt changes aspects of the wicked problem and even how the initial problem is understood and framed. This cause and effect potentially compound on itself, as attempts to correct previous solutions create more wicked problems, and the cycle repeats.

6. Wicked problems do not have an enumerable (i.e., an exhaustively describable) set of potential solutions, nor is there a well-described set of permissible operations that may be incorporated into the plan.

Because formulating the problem is part of the problem, there are also no definite criteria to identify when all possible solutions have been considered. "In such fields of ill-defined problems and hence ill-definable solutions, the set of feasible plans of action relies on realistic judgement, on the capability to appraise 'exotic' ideas and on the amount of trust and credibility . . . that will lead to the conclusion, 'OK let's try that.'"[77]

7. Every wicked problem is essentially unique.

Wicked problems cannot be grouped together into categories with pre-known, common solutions. While there may be similarities among

---

77. Rittel and Webber, "Dilemmas in a General Theory of Planning," 164.

wicked problems, there are still particularities that will significantly differentiate them from each other. Thus, one needs to be wary of applying solutions from one seemingly similar wicked problem to another. It may happen that the previous solution is totally incompatible due to unforeseeable differences between the wicked problems.

8. Every wicked problem can be considered a symptom of another wicked problem.

With tame problems, resolution involves looking for the underlying cause and then responding to it accordingly. For wicked problems, because of their interrelation with other problems, identifying the cause frequently unearths further wicked problems that need to be addressed.

9. The choice of explanation determines the nature of the problem's resolution.

Because of their complexity and indeterminacy, there is a certain level of arbitrariness in how wicked problems are explained. Because of the uniqueness of the problem, and the consequences that each solution generates, the way these problems are framed are due to what people think is plausible, fits their worldview and interests best, and appears to fit with viable solutions available.

10. The problem-solver has "no right to be wrong."

Every attempt to solve wicked problems counts since the consequences can have a huge and irreversible impacts on people and on the world. As such, people attempting to implement a solution have heavy responsibilities, since they are, to some degree, responsible, and liable for the consequences of their actions, whether foreseen or not. Rittel states this quite strongly: having "no right to be wrong" points to liability on the part of the design thinking practitioners for both short-term and long-term consequences. "Planners are liable for the consequences of the actions they generate: the effects can matter a great deal to those people that are touched by those actions."[78] At the same time, the rules do acknowledge the limitations of human beings, even when brought together as a group. This particular characteristic also implies the gravity of any project implemented in an attempt to solve a wicked problem. While human beings are certainly limited, design thinking practitioners cannot hide behind this

78. Rittel and Webber, "Dilemmas in a General Theory of Planning," 167.

limitation should extremely negative consequences happen, for which they may be held accountable by those affected, or by a government or other organization.

Business and economics, in particular, have many wicked problems that need to be dealt with, given the effects bad or good business and economics can have on a community. Many of these wicked problems are also structures of sin that keep people in unjust situations. To further illustrate these features of wicked problems, we can take a look at the problem of income inequality. Several bodies have stakes in this issue, including businesses, civil society, local communities, and government at both local and national level. Businesses are the primary stakeholders who provide the goods and services that generate income. Their actions directly affect the incomes of people and are directly affected by people's income, as well. On the one hand, the businesses are in direct control of the flow of income as they make decisions on the salary structures of their employees. On the other hand, income inequality affects businesses when their customers' purchasing power increases or decreases. Customers would generally prefer goods and services of lower price, which threatens the sales income of businesses. Businesses might then be tempted to produce cheaper products and services—at the expense of the salaries and wages of their employees. The end result is widening inequality.

There is no definitive formulation of the problem of income inequality because there is no simple equation or simple presentation of the numerous factors involved (feature 1). Various experts have suggested many causes of income inequality—these causes are interconnected, and even wicked problems in themselves (feature 8). There are multiple factors (feature 6), such as lack of access to quality education and healthcare, lack of sound policy on minimum wages, and problems with under- or unemployment because of lack of access to jobs (e.g., issues of urban planning or transport). Others note that with income inequality, there are people whose incomes cannot supply their needs, and they question whether products and services are affordable enough and accessible. Aside from working to close the gap in income inequality, ways to make goods and services affordable and accessible can also be developed.

Everything that has been mentioned about income inequality is also wicked problems. They are also complex issues that are difficult to solve; they themselves fit into Rittel and Webber's tenfold description. This is also the reason different people advocate different approaches to addressing income inequality. Some prioritize education, others examine the salary structures, some focus on providing access to jobs, and others advocate for more affordable products and services (feature 9). There are people who suggest small tweaks to businesses, while others argue for a complete overhaul of the ways in which business is conducted and the overarching economic system. Income inequality differs from area to area and would therefore require drastically different responses based on the area's culture, geography, and other relevant conditions (feature 7). For instance, one would require a different approach to income inequality in the United States and in the Philippines, due to the different cultures and systems present.

All these varied factors, coupled with the limited information available and limited nature of human beings, make it difficult to come up with a definitive solution that could solve income inequality. Responders to the issue also differ on what constitutes a solution (feature 2). Would solving income inequality mean everyone having the exact same income? Or would it mean everyone having enough for their basic needs and wants? If so, what distinguishes "needs" from "wants," and how would "enough" be measured?

Because of these complexities, limitations, and disagreements, any resolution put forward for income inequality could not be a once-and-for-all solution, but rather a proposal aimed towards simply improving the situation (feature 3). For example, if design thinking practitioners decide to implement a project in the area of education for traditional and nontraditional undergraduate students, then they're under the assumption that income inequality has its root primarily in the lack of opportunities for education. Depending on how education is delivered, such a project can cause a domino effect on other aspects of the community. It might also have unintended effects on the supply of people looking for work in a particular field. This can affect wages and prices, either improving or exacerbating income inequality. If this project focused on education beginning at earlier elementary levels, its unanticipated long-term effects would only become evident several years after the project was implemented (features 4 and 5).

Super Wicked Problems

Recent scholars have also proposed additional characteristics, especially in cases of what more researchers have identified as even more complex "super wicked problems." Pointing to the example of climate change, Kelly Levin et al., added the following criteria to the ten mentioned above:[79]

1. The problem has the additional constraint of time.

For a super wicked problem, there is an added urgency to the problem and time is running out. There are even more limited chances—or even none at all—of coming back to the beginning to try another approach. While other systems of problems are able to be "reset" to some degree, or at least return to a previous equilibrium, super wicked problems involve conditions that cannot be fully controlled.

2. Those who are causing and contributing to the problem are also those who are trying to look for a solution.

Super wicked problems also make it difficult, if not impossible, for people in today's structures to live without participating in some manner in these said structures. There are no passive observers in super wicked problems and there seems to be a degree of complicity even in the solutions that are presented. Every person who wishes to end climate change, for example, has contributed to climate change, including through the use of fossil fuels, which are used in cooking, transport, and creating various products and services.

3. Centralized forms of authority that may be needed to address such a problem are either weak or non-existent.

Because of the added layers of super wicked problems, identifying an authority, governing body, or centralized effort to address the problems might be impossible. The lack of centralized authority becomes a problem, especially when there are many stakeholders with varying and competing needs and interests. Coordination is important in responding to super wicked problems that require a global response, and such coordination is often difficult to do.

4. Policy responses often discount the future irrationally.

"Super wicked problems generate a situation in which the public and decision makers, even in the face of overwhelming evidence of the risks of or significant or even catastrophic impacts from inaction, make decisions

---

79. Levin et al., "Overcoming the Tragedy of Super Wicked Problems," 123–52.

that disregard this information and reflect very short-term horizons."[80] It is difficult for people and policy makers—who rely on the constituents' support and cooperation—to sacrifice the short-term for the sake of the long-term, even when knowing the risks of not doing so. At the same time, this inability or unwillingness to sacrifice for the long-term is exacerbated by the difficulty of predicting the exact outcomes of any one action.

    The climate crisis is another wicked problem where businesses are a primary stakeholder. Business operations are heavily affected by the climate crisis because it affects the availability of raw materials, and both inbound and outbound logistics of raw materials and finished products and services, respectively. At the same time, when businesses create products and services without addressing the sustainability of their products, the creation itself of the goods and disposal of waste can exacerbate the climate crisis. Income inequality and the climate crisis have a deeper link because prioritizing cheaper products and more affordable services results in businesses choosing to cut costs by utilizing more environmentally harmful resources and processes, such as more fossil fuels or more unrecyclable plastics. These interconnected wicked problems are the context in which businesses find themselves embedded as primary stakeholders. This is the context that needs to be addressed.

    By using the language of wicked problems, we can respond to the issue and think more systematically about what is keeping the structure of sin an ongoing issue, and how these drivers are related to each other. The language of wicked problems helps deconstruct the structure of sin to begin the process of identifying what tools, ideas, or solutions needed to address the structure in a systemic way.

CONCLUSION: STRUCTURES OF SIN AS WICKED PROBLEMS IN BUSINESS AS OPPORTUNITIES FOR DISRUPTION

Recent magisterial teaching made efforts to explain what structures of sin are, where they come from, and how such sinful structures affect human beings. While sin and its structures do not absolutely determine human beings, in treating these realities in such depth, magisterial teaching

---

80. Levin et al., "Overcoming the Tragedy of Super Wicked Problems," 128.

acknowledges a dynamic similar to that explained by Berger and Luckman. Human beings create these structures, but at the same time, are products of and affected by them. Catholic social teaching continues to identify the roots and perpetuation of these structures in the actions óf individuals, and often found them in vices such as greed or selfishness. These structures are complex webs of relationships which may amplify good or harm, similar to wicked problems. They may be symptomatic of each other, with high stakes involved, given their urgency and effects on the people and the environment.

In light of the documents and theologians discussed, the term "structure of sin" will be consistently used, distinguishing it from "social sin," in the same way Kelly differentiates the two terms by identifying structures of sin as a subspecies of social sin. A "structure of sin" in a business setting will be understood as: (1) a structure that violates human dignity by oppressing human beings and creating a power imbalance between an elite few and the rest of the relevant group or society; (2) "a situation that promotes individual selfishness" or the formation of vice in persons; or (3) a pattern of "habitual and unnoticed complicity or silent acquiescence when confronted with social injustice," such as the situations of moral complicity described by Barrera and Finn.[81]

The idea of structures of sin still requires further elaboration, however. The description of structural sin in magisterial documents may be helpful but they are not complete. It does not consider, for example, the ignorance that people may have. This ignorance leads to ethical blind spots that prevent people from understanding how systemic oppression operates invisibly and how it can be perpetuated even by the actions of the well-intentioned, which wicked problems also stress. For example, a consumer of Fair Trade products may act with the intention of promoting just business practices, based on the presence of the Fair Trade logo on products.[82]

However, because of the inconsistencies in the way the Fair Trade system is set up, a purchaser of Fair Trade branded goods may not, in actuality, be supporting a poor farmer, but rather enabling corrupt cooperatives or even harming other poor farmers.[83] Neither have official magisterial documents nor theologians and ethicists adequately accounted for the ways

81. Whitehead and Whitehead, "Attending to the Experience of Injustice," 128–29.
82. See Fair Trade International, "Fair Trade Standards."
83. See Griffiths, "Lack of Rigour in Defending Fairtrade," 103–4; Mendoza and Bastiaensen, "Fair Trade."

that good actions, despite best intentions, can still perpetuate structures of sin. With increasing complexities of markets, economics, and global relationships, the exploration of structures of sin also requires updating to continue accurately describing how contemporary structures manifest injustice and contribute to oppression or violence.

These structures of sin, or wicked problems, are opportunities for disruption. Their complexity and human centeredness highlight human agency as the core of why responding to the situation is difficult. Creation's dignity, and the interests and rights of both the human and natural world are not being heard or respected. These structures now become opportunities to address those rights and interests, to meet the unmet needs of many, as part of the work of building up the common good. They are also opportunities for disruption for smaller organizations that are often the ones that seek to change the status quo, since there is little impetus for those in power to change the way things are in the world. In business, smaller businesses are trying to create new ways of doing business through different modules, products, and services that are more sustainable or just.[84] They can be an example of seeing the structures of sin in business as a wicked problem, and responding to them through concrete business models and practices.

In order to respond effectively to the challenges posed by sinful structures in business and economy, ethicists and practitioners must do more than identify, denounce, or resist them. They must also be more purposeful in identifying, analyzing, and helping create the conditions for structures and systems. These systems make it easier to do the good in business, and easier to cultivate virtues and human flourishing. Magisterial teaching acknowledges that to respond to these structures, what is needed is not only individual action but also collective action, both at the grassroots level and at the level of larger institutions and public authorities. This is where design thinking, as a methodology, can strengthen the responses being crafted in business. It is an opportunity to change the way business is currently done, while also being enriched with further teaching on business and business ethics in Catholic social thought.

---

84. See Gallagher and Buckeye, *Structures of Grace*.

CHAPTER 2

Business and Business Ethics in Catholic Social Thought

MODERN CATHOLIC SOCIAL THOUGHT offers a worldview and principles that both illuminate and challenge underlying assumptions of the often-left unchallenged current business and economic systems. After Leo XIII's landmark encyclical *Rerum Novarum* issued in 1891, the tradition of modern social encyclicals, documents, homilies, and addresses from popes alongside magisterial statements has consistently addressed economic matters and offered broad principles applicable to business. The official social documents emphasize the dignity the Catholic Church has placed on the human person, the value of human labor, and the importance of justice in business and economic activity.

In the thirteen decades since *Rerum Novarum* and in the face of the changing economic landscape, the rapid pace of business life stoked by globalization, the use of the internet, and other advancing technology, Catholic Church leaders have voiced their concerns about various business and economic systems, namely, extreme neoliberal capitalism on one hand, or communism on the other that affect millions of people all over the world, not just materially by widening the gap between the rich and the poor, but also socially by promoting an exclusionary society where large numbers of people are marginalized.[1]

This chapter focuses on three particular principles and guidance that can be used for disrupting business and innovation towards the good: (1) both human dignity and creation's flourishing as important criteria for

1. See Badiou and Gauchet, *What Is to Be Done?*

judging whether a business is contributing to the common good; (2) the importance of subsidiarity on the one hand, the opportunity to participate in the business or the market, and solidarity on the other hand, acting with marginalized groups for whom participation is made difficult; (3) the importance of regulating bodies, usually the state, in ensuring that businesses and the economic system as a whole are at the service of humanity and creation. By the end of this chapter, we will have raised concerns on how Catholic social thought can be disruptive and how a dialogue on design thinking can address them.

BUSINESS ETHICS-RELATED PRINCIPLES AND THEMES IN MAGISTERIAL DOCUMENTS

While not all the magisterial documents have explicitly addressed business ethics per se, the issues tackled in the documents, such as workers' wages and rights, economic justice, and unions, are issues that also concern business ethics.

Rerum Novarum (1891)

Rerum Novarum is widely recognized as the first official papal encyclical in modern Catholic social teaching. In this papal encyclical, Leo XIII tackles issues including working conditions, rights, and wages. He exhorts business owners to reject exploitative working conditions and wages and instead give the workers their fair wages and ensure their safety and well-being in workplaces.[2] Leo XIII makes it clear that consent is a necessary but not sufficient part of ensuring that justice is given to the workers—"if through necessity or fear of a worse evil the workman accept harder conditions because an employer or contractor will afford him no better, he is made a victim of force and injustice."[3] In today's economic and political discourse, consent is often assumed to be the key factor in enforcing agreements or contracts and the main criterion in determining whether something is just. This is the main reason consent needs to be considered in this teaching. An institution, for example, might refuse to raise the low salaries of their

---

2. Shannon, *Commentary on Rerum Novarum*, loc. 4573–92, in Himes, *Modern Catholic Social Teaching*.

3. Leo XIII, *Rerum Novarum*, sec. 45.

workers, justifying it by using the signed agreements the workers agreed to in their contracts. Consent is therefore necessary, but not sufficient, to ensure that the work or situation is just.

In *Rerum Novarum*, Leo XIII appears hesitant in his acceptance of labor unions and unionizing, possibly because he emphasized harmony and non-adversarial relationships between workers and employers.[4] However, later magisterial documents would more strongly promote and support labor unions as a vital part of the business system. Because labor unions seek a balance of power, this ensures that workers are able to create a space to deal with conflict between the workers and employers through communication and negotiation.[5]

Quadragesimo Anno (1931), *Mater et Magistra* (1961), *Pacem in Terris* (1963), *Gaudium et Spes* (1965), and *Populorum Progressio* (1967)

In the century and a quarter after Leo XIII, various popes and synods of bishops added to Catholic social teaching on issues of development, urbanization, war and peace, justice, and other social issues, many of which are important to consider in business ethics. These concepts include a more robust definition of justice and the common good and their implications, as well as the idea of integral human development, compared to what Leo XIII discussed in *Rerum Novarum*.

First, Pius XI in *Quadragesimo Anno* offers a reflection on justice. He draws on Aristotle and Thomas Aquinas to describe three types of justice: distributive justice, contributive justice, and commutative justice. The first two forms of justice describe the relationship between individuals and the state: contributive justice labels the way individuals contribute resources to state and society, according to their ability. Distributive justice points to the state and society distributing the resources to individuals according

---

4. Shannon, *Commentary on Rerum Novarum*, loc. 4856–76.

5. As used in this work, the phrase "business systems and structures" encompasses processes within businesses that are used to achieve those business's objectives, as well as those in which the business finds itself embedded. Such systems include the socioeconomic and political situations they must navigate, such as the government agencies and structures businesses deal with to operate in a community, or the economic assumptions that undergird the community they are operating it, whether it be at the local or international level.

to need.⁶ Commutative justice or social justice is the form of justice that governs the relationship between individuals. The language of rights and duties, further elaborated in *Pacem in Terris*, is developed to identify how individuals are to relate to each other.⁷ These forms of justice describe the way the economy ought to work according to Catholic social thought, and situate businesses as helping ensure that distributive justice is enacted in a community.

Another idea discussed in the document is subsidiarity, a central concept that guides the vision of society described in Catholic social thought. Pius XI identifies the responsibility and power of the government, but such responsibility and power also have limits. For Pius XI, there is a particular order where the state "will more freely, powerfully, and effectively do all those things that belong to it alone because it alone can do them: directing, watching, urging, restraining, as occasion requires and necessity demands" while "let[ting] subordinate groups handle matters and concerns" that these subordinate groups are directly concerned with and can accomplish.⁸

Mater et Magistra and *Pacem in Terris* continue this focus on justice and further develop its relation to the idea of the common good. In *Mater et Magistra*, John XXIII highlights the role of government in ensuring that the vision of the common good is attained.⁹ Drawing from the work of Joseph Cardinal Cardijn, the methodology of putting Catholic social teaching into action can be described in three steps—to see, judge, and act.¹⁰ "First, one reviews the concrete situation; secondly, one forms a judgment on it in the light of these same principles; thirdly, one decides what in the circumstances can and should be done to implement these principles."¹¹

In his 1963 encyclical *Pacem in Terris*, John XXIII emphasizes the importance of rights and duties as part of just relationships between people, as well as the state's role in ensuring that these rights and duties are protected and the role individuals have in participating in the state.¹² *Pacem in Terris* continues what *Mater et Magistra* discussed on the growing interrelationship

---

6. Pius XI, *Quadragesimo Anno*, secs. 71, 75, 96.

7. Pius XI, *Quadragesimo Anno*, secs. 47–49.

8. Pius XI, *Quadragesimo Anno*, secs. 79–80.

9. John XXIII, *Mater et Magistra*, sec. 20.

10. Mich, *Commentary on Mater et Magistra*, loc. 7166–210, in Himes, *Modern Catholic Social Teaching*.

11. John XXIII, *Mater et Magistra*, sec. 236.

12. John XXIII, *Pacem in Terris*, secs. 8–79; Christiansen, "Commentary on *Pacem in Terris*," loc. 7842–903, in Himes, *Modern Catholic Social Teaching*.

between people and communities in its description of peoples' rights and corresponding duties. Concrete ways in the public sphere need to be identified to address the conflicts that arise from seeking the common good in such a plural and interdependent context.[13] Having an organization such as the United Nations (UN) is beneficial to promote international cooperation among countries, as well as the UN Declaration of Human Rights (UNDHR), which dovetail as well with the rights and goods outlined in sections 11–27 in *Pacem in Terris*.[14] The UNDHR has become the basis for the UN Principles of Responsible Management Education (UN PRME) and the UN Global Compact, both of which are used by business schools today to guide ethical business.

The Second Vatican Council's pastoral constitution "On the Church in the Modern World," *Gaudium et Spes*, issued in 1965, outlines the standard definition of the common good in the *Compendium of the Social Doctrine of the Catholic Church*.[15] This important conciliar document solidifies what previous encyclicals, beginning with *Rerum Novarum*, alluded to in using the term "common good":[16]

> Every day human interdependence grows more tightly drawn and spreads by degrees over the whole world. As a result the common good, that is, *the sum of those conditions of social life which allow social groups and their individual members relatively thorough and ready access to their own fulfillment*, today takes on an increasingly universal complexion and consequently involves rights and duties with respect to the whole human race. . . . At the same time, however, there is a growing awareness of the exalted dignity proper to the human person, since he stands above all things, and his rights and duties are universal and inviolable. Therefore, *there must be made available to all men everything necessary for leading a life truly human*, such as food, clothing, and shelter; the right to choose a state of life freely and to found a family, the right to education, to employment, to a good reputation, to respect, to appropriate information, to activity in accord with the upright norm of one's own conscience, to protection of privacy and rightful freedom even in matters religious.[17]

13. Christiansen, "Commentary on *Pacem in Terris*," loc. 7706.
14. John XXIII, *Pacem in Terris*, secs. 142–44.
15. Pontifical Council for Justice and Peace, *Compendium of the Social Doctrine of the Church*, sec. 164.
16. See Hollenbach, *Common Good and Christian Ethics*.
17. Second Vatican Council, *Gaudium et Spes*, sec. 26.

The common good assumes the fulfillment of a wide range of human rights. This includes both traditional political and civil rights, such as the right to free speech and assembly, but also includes social and economic rights, such as the right to adequate basic needs such as food, clothing, or shelter. While most countries' constitutions would guarantee the former, the latter may not necessarily be safeguarded in a legal way.

This definition of the common good also looks intently at the individual and the communal. These aspects of the common good are important because some may dismiss the common good as purely altruism, with no space for self-interest or concern, and thus is unrealistic. While there are costs to bear in bringing about the common good, there is a connection between the individual and the community since the development of one helps the development of all, and vice versa. It is thus not about uplifting the community at the expense of a particular person, but rather ensuring that conditions are available so that all may flourish and not just a few, and that any costs and risks are borne equitably.

In 1967, Paul VI, in *Populorum Progressio*, elaborates the important role that businesses play to ensure that fair trade relations and business dealings happen in developing countries.[18] Integral human development is also important because "the development we speak of here cannot be restricted to economic growth alone. To be authentic, it must be well rounded; it must foster the development of each man and of the whole man."[19] Paul VI continues to describe this development in terms of moving from "less than human conditions" towards "truly human conditions":

> What are less than human conditions [that oppose integral human development]? The material poverty of those who lack the bare necessities of life, and the moral poverty of those who are crushed under the weight of their own self-love; oppressive political structures resulting from the abuse of ownership or the improper exercise of power, from the exploitation of the worker or unjust transactions. What are truly human conditions [that comprise integral human development]? The rise from poverty to the acquisition of life's necessities; the elimination of social ills; broadening the horizons of knowledge; acquiring refinement and culture. From there one can go on to acquire a growing awareness of other people's dignity, a taste for the spirit of poverty, an active interest in the common good, and a desire for peace. . . . Finally,

---

18. Paul VI, *Populorum Progressio*, sec. 70.
19. Paul VI, *Populorum Progressio*, sec. 14.

and above all, there is faith—God's gift to men of good will—and our loving unity in Christ, who calls all men to share God's life as sons of the living God, the Father of all men.[20]

This concept of development is important in business ethics because it provides some of the backdrop assumptions of what might be a business's normative vision. This points to a vision of society and a certain standard of living to which businesses, through their operations, can help contribute towards. This includes not only material well-being, but also an awareness of one's interconnectedness with other creatures, both human and non-human, and a commitment towards serving the common good and contributing to genuine peace. This includes safeguarding not only political and civil rights, but also socioeconomic rights.

Laborem Exercens (1981) and *Sollicitudo Rei Socialis* (1987)

In these two documents, John Paul II further develops the treatment of work and solidarity. In *Laborem Exercens*, John Paul II emphasizes the dignity of work on the nintieth anniversary of *Rerum Novarum* and highlights that "*the primary basis of the value of work is man himself*, who is its subject. This leads immediately to a very important conclusion of an ethical nature: however true it may be that man is destined for work and called to it—work is 'for man' and not man 'for work.'"[21]

While people are called to work and to be creative through their work, work ought to be understood within the context of human dignity and the common good. He therefore calls for worker solidarity towards a "more committed realization by others of workers' rights. Workers can often share in running businesses and controlling their productivity, and they actually do. Through appropriate associations, they exercise influence over conditions of work and pay, and over social legislation. At the same time, various ideological or power systems and new relationships, which have arisen at various levels of society, *have allowed flagrant injustices to persist or have created new ones.*"[22]

Sollicitudo Rei Socialis develops this understanding of solidarity in light of authentic human development. According to John Paul II, "development, which is not only economic, must be measured and oriented

20. Paul VI, *Populorum Progressio*, sec. 21.
21. John Paul II, *Laborem Exercens*, sec. 6.
22. John Paul II, *Laborem Exercens*, sec. 8.

according to the reality and vocation of man seen in his totality." Authentic human development is therefore not simply about material well-being but also social, spiritual, and psycho-social well-being.[23] John Paul II thus invites people to commit to the "development of the whole human being and of all people" by improving working conditions and opportunities for employment, as well as reorienting society's attitude towards material wealth and property.[24]

Centesimus Annus (1991)

One hundred years after *Rerum Novarum*, John Paul II continues in *Centesimus Annus* the papal reflection on work in modern times. While conditions for work have become vastly different from what they were in the late-nineteenth century, he identifies that creating new challenges and issues, many of the same issues of justice in work, continue to oppress laborers. There is the importance of honoring the dignity of work in business and in the economy and acknowledging the "legitimate role of profit as an indication that a business is functioning well." However, the pope clarifies that profit is not and should not be the only criterion or metric to gauge a business's success—"other human factors must also be considered, which, in the long term, are at least equally important in the life of the business."[25] These other factors include the effects on environment and people, which will be further developed in *Caritas in Veritate* (2009) and *Vocation of the Business Leader* (2012).

With a nuanced description of businesses and their economic systems, John Paul II discussed both the positive and negative aspects of the form of business and capitalism predominant of the time. Business and capitalism can allow for an exercise of responsible freedom and creativity and become a viable a means for production and consumption of certain needs, but at the same time, unrestrained business and capitalism can also lead to consumerism and unequal wealth and power distribution, all of which can harm and marginalize people.[26] While John Paul II highlights communism and socialism's failures, he also makes clear that "socialism's failure does not

---

23. John Paul II, *Sollicitudo Rei Socialis*, sec. 29.
24. John Paul II, *Sollicitudo Rei Socialis*, sec. 30.
25. John Paul II, *Centesimus Annus*, sec. 34.
26. Finn, "Commentary on *Centesimus Annus*," loc. 15293–300, in Himes, *Modern Catholic Social Teaching*.

mean that a blind trust in the markets is now acceptable." He insists that a "proper economic system will be shaped by the preferential option for the poor which is to help entire peoples enter into productive economic life."[27]

Caritas in Veritate (2009)

Continuing the more explicit attention to business, in *Caritas in Veritate*, Benedict XVI focuses on the importance of questioning and regulating the systems and structures in which businesses are entrenched, since these systems and structures played a key role in the financial crisis of 2008 which wreaked economic harm on millions of people and households across numerous countries.[28]

Further developing the concepts of the common good and justice as inseparable from and intrinsic to charity, Benedict XVI argues that which concerns business's optimal operation in service of justice and the common good. More than just the logics of transactions and contracts, business and the market economy should include the "logic of gift."[29] This logic "does not exclude justice, nor does it merely sit alongside [justice] as a second element added from without; [rather] economic, social, and political development [including commercial relationships], if it is to be authentically human, needs to make room for the principle of gratuitousness as an expression of fraternity."[30]

The market should be a space for people to exchange goods and services needed and the market's mechanisms require trust and solidarity. It is only through this logic, together with solidarity and trust, that the market can function properly, and all three forms of justice can be realized in business and the economy. Benedict XVI notes that business "cannot concern itself only with the interests of the proprietors, but must also assume responsibility for all the other stakeholders who contribute to the life of the business: the workers, the clients, the suppliers of various elements or production, the community of reference."[31] A business should consciously operate in how it affects not just the people who have a direct financial stake in the organization, but also those who are indirectly connected to

---

27. Finn, "Commentary on *Centesimus Annus*," loc. 15293, 15306.
28. Hinze, "Economic Recession, Work, and Solidarity," 150–69.
29. Benedict XVI, *Caritas in Veritate*, secs. 34–35.
30. Benedict XVI, *Caritas in Veritate*, sec. 34.
31. Benedict XVI, *Caritas in Veritate*, sec. 40.

the business's operations, and include attention to these other stakeholders in the business's strategic plans and vision.

Towards Reforming the International Financial and Monetary Systems in the Context of the Global Public Authority (2011)

Continuing *Caritas in Veritate*'s commentary on the economic system and the ways in which it ought to be reformed, the Pontifical Council for Justice and Peace released a document in 2011 on the need for an ethical framework to circumscribe the overall economic system. The prevailing technocracy concentrates power and wealth among the few. There is a strong need not only for technological advances in the way financial instruments are used and developed, but also for an ethics that is directed towards the common good.

To move in this direction, there are two important factors needed: (1) a way to stabilize money supply; and (2) a "minimum shared body of rules to manage the global financial market, which has grown much more rapidly than the real economy."[32] Governments and businesses are advised to create regulation on such matters as: "1) taxation measures on financial transactions; 2) the use of public funds in bank recapitalization; and 3) the use of and rules surrounding ordinary credit and investment banking."[33]

Vocation of the Business Leader (2012)

From the macroeconomic level, we move to the micro level directed at individuals engaging in business. The *Vocation of the Business Leader*, issued in 2012 with the fifth edition issued in 2018 by the Pontifical Council for Justice and Peace (now the Dicastery for Promoting Integral Human Development) uses previous documents to reflect on how to do business with ethical principles and Christian values. A business's aim, from this perspective, is to create goods and services that actually serve the needs of people. It is also to provide work that is life-giving and allows people to be creative as well as support themselves and their families. Its aim is to also

---

32. Pontifical Council for Justice and Peace, *Towards Reforming Financial and Monetary Systems*.

33. Pontifical Council for Justice and Peace, *Towards Reforming Financial and Monetary Systems*.

provide wealth that is equitably distributed and to ensure that resources are responsibly used.[34]

In *Vocation of the Business Leader*, the purpose of business and the responsibilities of the business person are identified by naming six principles that govern the creation of good goods, good work, and good wealth that are in line with the common good. These six principles related to goods, work, and wealth that can guide businesses in this direction draw on the fundamental themes in modern Catholic social teaching.[35]

Good Goods

Principle 1: "Businesses *contribute to the common good* by producing goods that are truly good and services that truly serve."

"Successful businesses identify and seek to address genuine human needs at a superior level of excellence using a great deal of innovation." To serve the common good, "the goods and services that businesses produce should . . . include things with clear social value—such as lifesaving medical devices, microfinance, education, social investment, fair trade products, renewable energy, artistic enterprises, health care, or affordable housing. It also includes anything that contributes to human development and fulfillment while caring for our common home."[36] This principle identifies concrete contributions to human development as constituting part of the "sum total of conditions" needed for people to flourish.

Principle 2: "Businesses maintain *solidarity* with the poor by being alert for opportunities to serve deprived and underserved populations and people in need and removing obstacles that prevent the excluded from participating in the economy."

Drawing directly from John Paul II's social teachings, solidarity is understood as "not a feeling of vague compassion or shallow distress at the misfortunes of so many people, both near and far. On the contrary, it is a firm and persevering determination to commit oneself to the common

---

34. Dicastery for Promoting Integral Human Development, "Vocation of the Business Leader."

35. Dicastery for Promoting Integral Human Development, "Vocation of the Business Leader," 18.

36. Dicastery for Promoting Integral Human Development, "Vocation of the Business Leader," 13.

good; that is to say to the good of all and of each individual, because we are all really responsible for all."[37] Thus, to be in solidarity with the poor and other marginalized communities, businesses need to work intentionally towards their well-being as part of the common good. Putting this understanding of the common good in to practice in creating goods and services, the business people are encouraged to create goods and services that can help "lift people from extreme poverty [and] spark their creativity and entrepreneurship and contribute to launching a dynamic of development."[38]

Good Work

Principle 3: "Businesses make a contribution to the community by fostering the special *dignity of human work*."

Drawing from *Centesimus Annus* and *Laborem Exercens*, *Vocation of the Business Leader* opposes the kind of alienated labor that treats people simply as cogs in the corporate machine.[39] Business people need to be reminded that work is an integral part of human existence. It is not simply about production or acquiring the means to material survival, but also about the development and flourishing of the human person through their work activity.

Principle 4: "Businesses that embrace *subsidiarity* provide opportunities for employees to exercise their gifts as they contribute to the mission of the organization."

This principle dovetails with what business people might know as "empowerment" through participatory workplaces. This is a principle that emphasizes that people "develop best in work when [they] use [their] gifts and freedom to achieve shared goals and to create sustain right relationships with one another. In other words, the more participatory the workplace, the more likely all workers will be to develop their gifts and talents . . . this fosters initiative, innovation, creativity, and a sense of shared responsibility."[40]

---

37. John Paul II, *Sollicitudo Rei Socialis*, sec. 38.

38. Dicastery for Promoting Integral Human Development, "Vocation of the Business Leader," 14.

39. See John Paul II, *Laborem Exercens*, sec. 6.

40. Dicastery for Promoting Integral Human Development, "Vocation of the Business Leader," 16.

Business and Business Ethics in Catholic Social Thought

Good Wealth

Principle 5: "Businesses model *stewardship* of the resources under their control—whether capital, human or environmental—in order to take care of humanity's common social and natural home."

Stewardship has appeared in Catholic social thought as one model of human beings interacting with the rest of creation. This particular paradigm rejects an understanding of human beings as dominating and exploiting the rest of creation.[41] In stewardship's understanding of humans' relationship with the natural world, the "human role . . . is one of care and service, exercised on behalf of God and with accountability to God."[42] Based on the stewardship model, this fifth principle knows the importance of a business's viability, and the importance of maintaining a reasonable profit through an efficient use of resources. Efficiency does not just mean attaining the most profit at the least cost, but rather, the ability to conduct one's business operations in a sustainable way that does not deplete the resources upon which a business depends (whether capital, human, or environmental resources).

Principle 6: "Businesses are *just* in the allocation of benefits to all stakeholders (employees, customers, investors, suppliers, and the community) and in how they bear the costs of their business operations."

A just distribution of whatever wealth business creates in its operations is quite important, drawing on the argument *Caritas in Veritate* makes on wealth distribution.[43] While profit is often distributed primarily through dividends for shareholders who have a monetary stake in the business, the understanding of justice presented in this principle aims to broaden the definition of the stakeholders of the business; employees, customers, and the local community, for example, are other stakeholders as well. Business people need to reflect on who truly shoulders the costs of the business's operations, and how the costs are actually distributed across the different stakeholders.

---

41. See Benedict XVI, *Caritas in Veritate*, sec. 50.

42. See Bauckham, *Bible and Ecology*, 2; Zenner, "Commentary on *Laudato Si*'," loc. 17866–90, in Himes, *Modern Catholic Social Teaching*.

43. Benedict XVI, *Caritas in Veritate*, secs. 32–42.

Evangelii Gaudium (2013), *Laudato Si'* (2015), and *Laudato Deum* (2023)

In *Evangelii Gaudium* ("Apostolic Exhortation on the Proclamation of the Gospel Today"), published during the first year of his pontificate, Francis critiques "the prevailing economic system" and the role businesses have in the said system, charging them with exclusion of and violence against the poor.[44] He connects this problem of exclusion and violence to the problem of environmental degradation in *Laudato Si'* ("On Care for Our Common Home"), his 2015 encyclical.[45] In *Evangelii Gaudium*, the "noble vocation" of business is to provide for the needs of people and help people flourish. Francis continues his predecessors' emphasis on integral human development and states that "growth in justice requires more than economic growth, while presupposing such growth: it requires decisions, programs, mechanisms, and processes specifically geared to a better distribution of income, the creation of sources of employment and an integral promotion of the poor, which goes beyond a simple welfare mentality."[46]

In light of Francis's comprehensive vision of development, *Laudato Si'* strongly criticizes businesses that focus on economic growth and profit maximization alone to the detriment of all else, including other human beings and the environment:

> The principle of the maximization of profits, frequently isolated from other considerations, reflects a misunderstanding of the very concept of the economy. As long as production is increased, little concern is given to whether it is at the cost of future resources or the health of the environment; as long as the clearing of a forest increases production, no one calculates the losses entailed in the desertification of the land, the harm done to biodiversity or the increased pollution.[47]

Francis emphasizes more strongly than any of his predecessors the importance of the environment. He cites the need for great ecological sensitivity, alongside care for human dignity. He also warns against "power structures based on the techno-economic paradigm" as such power structures, he

---

44. Francis, *Evangelii Gaudium*, secs. 53–54.
45. Francis, *Evangelii Gaudium*, secs. 59–60; Francis, *Laudato Si'*, secs. 138–40.
46. Francis, *Evangelii Gaudium*, sec. 204.
47. Francis, *Laudato Si'*, sec. 195.

contends, would lead to an erosion of freedom and justice in economics.[48] This paradigm is an overexerting control over nature and people—it "exalts the concept of a subject who, using logical and rational procedures, progressively approaches and gains control over an external object" or people.[49] These themes continue in *Laudato Deum*, where Francis emphasizes the role that businesses and business leaders have in shaping the agenda and plans of businesses to address the current climate crisis.[50]

His teaching on integral ecology links environmental and social justice together, and it criticizes certain current structures in business and economics that harm not just human beings but also the environment. He rejects the way businesses profit from the environment without paying the needed costs to replace and sustain the resources that have been used. Businesses need to be transparent in how they identify the environmental costs they bear.

Considerations for an Ethical Discernment Regarding Some Aspects of the Present Economic-Financial System: *Oeconomicae et Pecuniariae Quaestiones* (2018)

In 2018, the Vatican Dicastery for Promoting Integral Human Development issued a document concerning financial markets addressing the issues of extreme wealth inequality previously discussed in *Evangelii Gaudium* and *Laudato Si'*. The document speaks of the need for a "new economy" to replace the present neoliberal capitalist system. Section five in this document states:

> The recent financial crisis might have provided the occasion to develop a new economy, more attentive to ethical principles, and a new regulation of financial activities that would neutralize predatory and speculative tendencies and acknowledge the value of the actual economy. Although there have been many positive efforts at various levels which should be recognized and appreciated, there does not seem to be any inclination to rethink the obsolete criteria that continue to govern the world.[51]

---

48. Francis, *Laudato Si'*, sec. 53.
49. Francis, *Laudato Si'*, secs. 106–14.
50. Francis, *Laudate Deum*, secs. 10, 60.
51. Dicastery for Promoting Integral Human Development, *Oeconomicae et Pecuniariae Quaestiones*.

To this end, there is the need to advance: (1) new criteria to measure well-being and progress, as opposed to simply using a country's Gross Domestic Product (GDP); (2) holistic business education that situates business as a profession that aims to help people achieve holistic well-being and not just financial well-being; and (3) greater cooperation among all the agents within the economic and financial system.[52]

Final Document of the Amazon Synod (2019), *Querida Amazonia* (2020), and *Fratelli Tutti* (2020)[53]

Citing *Laudato Si'* and affirming the Final Document of the Amazon Synod, in his post-synodal exhortation *Querida Amazonia*, Francis reminds people of the power imbalances present in current economic and political structures. He points particularly to the "colonizing interests" of certain industries in the region that have contributed to economic migration and the climate crisis.[54] He warns against globalization becoming the new face of colonization, where multinational businesses or foreign organizations profit at the expense of the marginalized in "economic relationships . . . [that] become an instrument of death."[55]

In his 2020 social encyclical *Fratelli Tutti*, Francis continues to reiterate the important roles that business has in ensuring the common good. Businesses "should always be clearly directed to the development of others and to eliminating poverty, especially through the creation of diversified work opportunities."[56] He highlights the need for "business creativity" in the economy in order to ensure that jobs may be created, not cut in the wake of the COVID-19 pandemic, and that people may continue to be able to meet their basic needs.[57]

---

52. Dicastery for Promoting Integral Human Development, *Oeconomicae et Pecuniariae Quaestiones*, secs. 10–11, 20–24.
53. Synod of Bishops for the Pan-Amazon, *Final Document of the Amazon Synod*.
54. Francis, *Querida Amazonia*, sec. 9.
55. Francis, *Querida Amazonia*, sec. 14.
56. Francis, *Fratelli Tutti*, sec. 123.
57. Francis, *Fratelli Tutti*, sec. 168.

BUSINESS ETHICS-RELATED PRINCIPLES AND THEMES IN SELECT CATHOLIC THEOLOGIANS' WORK

Various Catholic philosophers and theologians have written on issues pertinent to business ethics, drawing from the principles mentioned above and Catholic theology in general.[58] In the U.S., priest-economist Monsignor John A. Ryan wrote in the early twentieth century on the issues of capital, economic rent and interest, profit in business, and the proper "just share" of profit for the business person.[59] His ideas have contributed significantly to the discussions of work and wage justice.

While aware of the difficulties and complexities of his proposals, Ryan argues the importance of a living wage, i.e., the minimum return due to workers that allows a person to receive enough sustenance for their self and family.[60] He offers several ways to compute a just living wage, and, in addition, deals with the broader problem of alienated labor. He pushes for a move towards an industrial democracy that minimizes alienated labor by sharing power with workers through more worker participation in managerial decisions.

Christine Hinze brings Ryan's work to bear on the situation of the twenty-first century working family in the United States and fills in the gaps of Ryan's work. Paying careful attention to "intersecting-, power and difference-related dynamics" such as race, class, and gender, Hinze fleshes out what she calls an ethic of "radical sufficiency," the foundation of a "contemporary Catholic livelihood agenda."[61] For Hinze, a "radical sufficiency livelihood agenda presses those struggling for work justice to take into account and responsibly address both the inequities of gender, race, and class, and the looming ecological crisis," to create space for all to participate and "gain access to enough," and attend to both actionable incremental solutions and deep systemic changes needed.[62]

Writing between the 1990s and 2010s, Catholic business ethicists Michael Naughton and Gene Laczniak uses Church documents and Scripture to present a theology of work and the implications of the Gospel on work and human dignity in business.[63] Their work continues many of

---

58. See Schlag and Melé, *Catholic Spirituality for Business*.
59. Ryan, *Distributive Justice*.
60. Ryan, *Economic Justice*.
61. Hinze, *Radical Sufficiency*, 70–71.
62. Hinze, *Radical Sufficiency*, 265–66.
63. Naughton and Laczniak, "Theological Context of Work," 981–94.

the themes already present in Ryan's writings on fair work and wages, and further develops the idea of distributive justice. They apply these ideas to various parts of the business value chain, in particular, in marketing.[64]

Naughton, together with Kenneth Goodpaster, Jeanne Buckeye, and Dean Maines, also authored a document in 2015, after the 2012 edition of *The Vocation of the Business Leader*, that focuses on bringing in subsidiarity to the workplace.[65] Theological ethicist Christina McRorie expresses that ethicists should pay more attention to the ways in which economic markets—spaces wherein "an agent is making a decision among various options with regard to a financial matter"—are moral architectures that can improve or impede people's development as moral agents.[66] Using behavioral economics, McRorie's work shows how the market's architecture can influence the choices, preferences, habits, and decision-making processes of individuals, and by extension, the businesses embedded in the architecture as well. Businesses are therefore not just neutrally satisfying the needs and wants of consumers but themselves affected by the larger moral architecture.

In the realm of humanistic business management, business ethicist Domènec Melé has contributed to the theological anthropology that underpins business and economics—an important aspect of understanding and developing ethical business practices in business governance and organizational development.[67] His work focuses on Catholic social thought to provide concrete principles and practices that can help businesses orient themselves more towards the well-being of people. Business ethicist Michael Pirson uses case studies on a variety of topics in business, such as sustainability and globalization. Pirson also incorporates the themes of dignity, social innovation, and well-being that are central to Catholic social thought.[68]

---

64. Laczniak et al., "On the Nature of 'Good' Goods," 125–29.
65. Naughton et al., "Respect in Action."
66. McRorie, "Markets as Moral Architectures."
67. Melé, "Firm as a 'Community of Persons,'" 89–101; Melé and Cantón, "*Homo Economicus* Model," 9–29.
68. See Pirson, "Humanistic Perspective for Management Theory," 39; Pirson et al., "Social Innovation and the Future of Business and Business Education," 1–6; Pirson et al., "Dignity and the Process of Social Innovation," 1–29.

KEY THEMES IN CATHOLIC SOCIAL THOUGHT

Catholic social thought has developed many helpful insights for business ethics. Its strong focus on the dignity of the human person underpins many of the key themes developed in its documents, such as the dignity of work and the concepts of solidarity, justice, and the common good. Late in the twentieth century, other timely topics were included in other documents, such as care for the environment and stronger support for unions and grassroots organizing. These later documents began to focus on economics or work in general and on business organizations and the ways in which businesses conduct themselves in relation to individual consumers, civil society, and public authority. On the one hand, these developments have served as guiding principles for many business people who wish to bring together their Christian faith commitment and their work.[69] On the other hand, it is difficult to apply these principles in new and emerging complex contexts where the business landscape is becoming more competitive and cutthroat, especially since the focus in business ethics has been on the individual, and not on changing the systems and structures that make it difficult to do the good.[70]

Several important themes emerge from this discussion and the theologians who have engaged with them. These are the important themes and principles that must guide the ways business are conducted, in particular: (1) both human dignity and creation's flourishing as important criteria for judging whether a business is contributing to the common good; (2) the importance of subsidiarity on the one hand, (i.e., the opportunity to participate in the business or the market), and, solidarity on the other (i.e., acting with marginalized groups for whom participation is made difficult); and (3) the importance of regulating bodies, usually the state, in ensuring that businesses and the economic system as a whole are at the service of humanity and creation.

---

69. See Sadowski, "Business Leaders Explore Ways to Carry Catholic Values to the Office." Other organizations include the Economy of Communion, under the guidance of the Focolare movement, and UNIAPAC, a network of Christian business leaders.

70. See Gentile, *Giving Voice to Values*.

Human Dignity and the Common Good

First, upholding human dignity, creation's sustainability, and their flourishing together are important measures of whether or not a business is just and working towards the common good. A qualitative assessment of whether business contributes to the better living conditions of human beings augments the quantitative metrics of profit and market values as criteria for what a good business looks like. While acknowledging the validity of profit, growth, and financial data as measures of business performance, it is clear that these criteria cannot be used as the sole metric of a "good business." Instead, a viewpoint oriented by Catholic social thought insists on including other indicators—not just monetary—for human well-being and ensures that distributive justice is served alongside commutative and contributive justice. There is also a stronger call for care of the environment and not just as the source of raw materials for business operations. More importantly, it also because of its inherent value as part of the community of creation within which the business—and the human beings—are embedded. Such a viewpoint is espoused in the concept of integral human development, which highlights the holistic nature of our flourishing, and that flourishing is of both the individual and society.

Both the individual and community are highlighted here. The extreme of selfish individualism that only focuses on the self is rejected, as well as the other extreme of total collectivism that sacrifices the individual's agency and gifts in the name of community. Both human dignity and the common good are balanced in doing good business, especially when it comes to evaluating and remunerating the labor that people bring into keeping a business running.

Subsidiarity and Solidarity

Second, solidarity and subsidiarity are important guiding principles that businesses must consider in their operations. Solidarity is that commitment to the common good, practiced through businesses offering good and service that support people and the environment, rather than harm them. Profit is a key part of keeping a business afloat. It can tempt many business owners to sacrifice the environment and people in exchange for short term profits. Rather than the long-term concerns of keeping the environment and people healthy and flourishing, the quick money and intense focus on growth as an indicator of what a good business is makes businesses forego solidarity. Catholic social thought warns against such short-term thinking and the emphasis on the idea of limitless growth. Instead, it reminds businesses of the importance of solidarity in ensuring the long-term gains of all involved—the environment, the people, and the business.

Commitment to advancing the common good (i.e., solidarity) is reflected in creating products of good quality in response to genuine human needs as well as ensuring a space for people to participate in business and the market economy actively and equitably (i.e., subsidiarity), whether through access to particular goods and services, or access to decent work that provides safe working conditions and a living wage. Working towards the vision of society as one that is marked with solidarity and the common good entails practicing subsidiarity.[71]

This commitment requires a special attention to the most vulnerable and marginalized. The common good is not just the good of many or majority but includes the good of those most often forgotten in society. Allowing smaller businesses to participate in the global market and supply chain, rather than buying them out and consolidating power among a few conglomerates, is another way of practicing subsidiarity. Solidarity and subsidiarity invite businesses to reflect on the vulnerable and marginalized groups as either customers who need to be served or a possible partner in business. They are not to be exploited as gullible customers, opportunities for advertisements, or cheap labor, but rather the aim is to create more inclusive business that genuinely serves everyone in the community.

Structures and Regulating Bodies in Business

Third, the documents stress the proper and necessary role that government and other authoritative bodies have in regulating the market systems within which businesses engage, while staunchly rejecting any form of authoritarianism, populism, or totalitarianism. One should be concerned with the structures at work in the world that affect businesses, and not just individual behavior or attitudes, hence the focus on structures of sin and structures of grace or solidarity in business and economics.[72] Markets cannot be left alone to their own devices or to the so-called "invisible hand," especially in

---

71. Pontifical Council for Justice and Peace, *Compendium of the Social Doctrine of the Church*, sec. 189.

72. Pontifical Council for Justice and Peace, *Compendium*, sec. 511.

assuring the delivery of certain products, resources, or outcomes that are deemed human rights, such as education and healthcare. The state and civil society, alongside other institutions, have a role in shaping business practices, products, and services to be in line with the common good, especially in ensuring that human dignity and the common good are protected.

Theological ethicist Daniel Finn clarifies in his work on the moral ecology of markets that "the key insight . . . is that the economic defense of self-interest—whether by Adam Smith or by contemporary positions across the political spectrum—does not simply claim that acting in one's own interest is just regardless of context. It is just or moral only if the context is the right one, a judgement that requires both moral analysis and extensive social scientific investigation of the cultural and institutional situation. The economic defense of self-interest is conditional, and the conditions matter a great deal."[73] Heavily influenced by the institutions mentioned above, their structures and policies can encourage businesses to go in particular decisions. Thus, these bigger bodies, without stepping on the opportunities and needs of the smaller organizations, need to be carefully considered, and their work scrutinized, in relation to how they contribute to the protection of human dignity and the common good.

CONCLUSION: PRINCIPLES OF CATHOLIC SOCIAL THOUGHT AS DISRUPTION

This chapter has taken an extensive look at the key concepts for Catholic social thought that are useful for business ethics and disrupting the way business is done. Catholic social thought offers a range of resources and principles for thinking about business and its structures plus offers guidance on the direction that disruptive innovation should move in. Disruptive innovation must be grounded in care for human dignity and the common good and committed to these two principles through solidarity and subsidiarity. This ideally comes from both the top (i.e., larger institutions) and the bottom (i.e., smaller organizations or groups) with larger institutions regulating and synergizing resources and efforts and harnessing these towards the flourishing of creation. However, disruption often happens from grassroots and smaller organizations, who provide more concrete and important insights that those at the top or in larger institutions may not necessarily see or know given their particular position.

73. Finn, *Moral Ecology of Markets*, 148.

There are, however, several concerns that need to be raised in this effort of disrupting business using Catholic social thought. First, while Catholic social thought offers the vision of flourishing as a goal for creation alongside broad moral principles to consider, the specific question of how organizations can translate principles into concrete structures and solutions that would disrupt business needs to be more fully addressed. Identifying the criteria and rubrics that can help guide businesses that wish to operate in a manner consistent with Catholic social thought—or as businesses might understand it, with justice or humanistic management—are required. For example, while Catholic social thought critiques the use of profit margins as the primary indicator of a business or economy performance, viable alternatives are yet to be promoted, leaving unanswered questions. More steps need to be done to present alternative criteria for new ways of organizing businesses, its systems, and structures, and for evaluating their success.

Second, it is still inescapable that the language, terms, and tools used in Catholic social thought are unfamiliar to the business world. Most people in business neither understand nor even know about Catholic social thought, much less find it a compelling source or interlocutor. At the same time, theologians do not necessarily comprehend business and the way it works in detail and in its totality. The task of the Catholic social ethicist begins with making Catholic social thought understandable and credible to other disciplines outside of theology. This entails not only translating terms into "business speak" but, more fundamentally, making a case for the relevance of Catholic social thought to business people who may have fears and concerns, for instance, about the religious specificity or dimensions of what this tradition proposes in the context of the pluralistic world. Making this case includes explaining the fundamental similarities and differences between the aims of Catholic social thought and mainstream economics and articulating in persuasive ways what Catholic social thought can offer to mainstream economics and business to improve their analyses and activities. Parallel to this, Catholic scholars and practitioners will be more effective in this endeavor if they, in turn, understand and use can learn to understand and effectively use the language and concepts of business and economics.

Third, Catholic social teaching has tended to depict processes of change—a big part of disruptive innovation—as simple, and that conflict in the process is treated as negative. Catholic social thought offers broad principles and frameworks that, at times, seem to suggest that social change is a harmonious and neat process that comes from the top and trickles down to the bottom. It is not. Rather, it is a slow, iterative, and often messy process that allows for initiatives from the bottom that influence the top.[74] In particular, modern Catholic social teaching has tended to downplay, and therefore underestimate, the role of conflict in both ethical decision-making and in the dynamics of structures, especially when changes are underway in a particular organization. Promoting harmony and peace has been a central concern in Catholic social teaching, whether it be peace among classes in *Rerum Novarum* or among nations in *Populorum Progressio*. Yet change and conflict are inevitable in social and organizational life, especially when resources or manpower are scarce. It is therefore important for theological ethicists, including business ethicists, to develop frameworks and ways of proceeding that effectively navigate conflict in business decision-making.

These concerns point to the need for resources and tools that can assist in establishing conditions for and conversations between the fields of business ethics and Catholic social thought. They need to be substantive, constructively critical, and mutually beneficial in the work of disruption and innovation. Given the concerns above, we will discuss one invaluable resource for disruption and innovation in business called design thinking, a rich dialogue partner for Catholic social thought in doing better business, in the next chapter.

---

74. See Leo XIII, *Rerum Novarum*, secs. 16, 36, 55; John XXIII, *Pacem in Terris*, secs. 80–125; Curran, *Catholic Social Teaching*, 86–89.

CHAPTER 3

Responding to Wicked Problems with Design Thinking

WE TURN TO A language familiar to business people and designers: the language of design thinking in response to wicked problems in business. The method of design thinking became popular in the 1990s among business people through IDEO, a well-known consultancy based in the United States, which has been a pioneer in practicing design thinking since the late 1970s.[1] Used for product and value chain innovation, design thinking has also been adapted to address problems in civil organizations, such as the work of Jeanne Liedtka, professor of Business Administration at the University of Virginia. She offers various case studies wherein principles for design thinking and innovation are employed in the social sector, which includes health, education, and other non-profit and non-governmental organizations.[2]

What is design thinking? What is its methodology, its limitations, and the principles that animate its process towards more ethical and good disruption? This chapter highlights the potential of this dialogue for illuminating both business and Catholic ethics participants' understanding of structures of sin. This dialogue will equip them to envisage and enact strategies for becoming "disruptors" that move business towards structures of grace.

---

1. See http://www.ideo.com.
2. Liedtka et al., *Design Thinking for the Greater Good*.

DESIGN THINKING

The "design" in design thinking refers to the construction and development of systems, structures, or artifacts that are not just aesthetically pleasing, but also functional and meaningful to the user. Austrian-American designer Victor Papanek points out:

> Any attempt to separate design, to make it a thing-by-itself, works counter to the inherent value of design as the primary underlying matrix of life. Design is composing an epic poem, executing a mural, painting a masterpiece, writing a concerto. But design is also cleaning and reorganizing a desk drawer, pulling an impacted tooth, baking an apple pie, choosing sides for a back-lot baseball game, and educating a child.[3]

Papanek, who was conscious of his work's social and environmental impact, maintained that in design thinking, "design is the conscious effort to impose meaningful order . . . design must be meaningful."[4] Similar to the common good in Catholic social thought, design in design thinking orders relationships and priorities towards something good for people. For design thinking advocates, design is crucial for understanding the world because the ways that systems and structures are designed—whether in business, the sciences, or the arts—have an effect in shaping human experience. People also encounter symbolic and visual language in their everyday interactions with other people and when they encounter objects in different social sites. These, too, are affected by design, whether consciously or unconsciously. "All that we do, almost all the time, is design for design is basic to all human activity. The planning and patterning of any act towards a desired, foreseeable end constitutes the design process."[5]

Design thinking takes this definition of design and its implications and uses it to understand and more effectively construct the products, systems, and services used by and embedded in humans. As design thinking expert Bruce Nussbaum puts it, "the contributions of Design Thinking to the field of design and to society at large are immense. By formalizing the tacit values and behaviors of design, Design Thinking was able to move designers and the power of design [within business] from a focus on artifact and aesthetics within a narrow consumerist marketplace to the much wider

---

3. Papanek, *Design for the Real World*, 1, 5.
4. Papanek, *Design for the Real World*, 5.
5. Papanek, *Design for the Real World*, 1.

social space of systems and society."⁶ In our contemporary globalizing context, he continues, "we face huge forces of disruption, the rise and fall of generations, the spread of social media technologies, the urbanization of the planet, the rise and fall of nations, global warming, and overpopulation. Together these forces are eroding our economic, social, and political systems in a once-in-a-century kind of way." At this pivotal moment in history, where so many historical shifts are happening with various social and environmental impacts, Nussbaum concludes, "Design Thinking [has] made design system-conscious."⁷

Design thinking can have many definitions and models, depending on the organization in which it is being employed. Tim Brown, CEO and president of IDEO, describes design thinking as "tap[ping] into capacities we all have but are overlooked by more conventional problem-solving practices . . . rely[ing] on our ability to be intuitive, to recognize patterns, to construct ideas that have emotional meaning as well as functionality." For Brown, design thinking "is a fundamentally exploratory process."⁸ Design thinking is understood as a problem-solving methodology that approaches and understands complex social problems as rooted in human beings' complex identities, relationships, and decisions. Design thinking practitioners approach problems as "human centered, possibility driven, option focused, and iterative."⁹

Liedtka offers a succinct explanation of each characteristic: first, "human-centered [means that] design thinking emphasizes the importance of deep exploration into the lives and problems of people whose lives we want to improve *before* we start generating solutions. . . . [I]t is enthusiastic about the potential to reframe our definition of the problem and engage stakeholders in co-creation."¹⁰ Second, being possibility driven and option focused means "generating multiple options and [avoiding] putting all our eggs in one particular solution basket."¹¹ This is especially necessary because there are typically many conflicting needs among stakeholders, as well as needs that may not be explicitly stated or even known to the stakeholders. Lastly, design thinking is iterative because it "conducts cycles of real world

---

6. Nussbaum, *Design Thinking Is a Failed Experiment*, para. 7.
7. Nussbaum, *Design Thinking Is a Failed Experiment*, para. 7.
8. Brown, *Change by Design*, 10, 22.
9. Liedtka et al., *Design Thinking for the Greater Good*, 6.
10. Liedtka et al., *Design Thinking for the Greater Good*, 6.
11. Liedtka et al., *Design Thinking for the Greater Good*, 6.

experiments to refine ideas, rather than running analyses using historical data. We don't expect to get it right the first time—we expect to iterate our way to success."[12]

Design thinking offers a way forward in responding to such complex situations as described in wicked problems. Comprised of a particular mindset together with its particular methodology and guiding principles, design thinking's goal is to help its practitioners creatively respond to situations that meet the criteria for wicked problems described earlier.

While the literature of design thinking outlines several detailed steps when describing the methodology of design thinking,[13] actual practitioners do not treat these steps as a simple recipe to be followed to the dot in order to achieve results. Due to the nature of wicked problems, it is simply impossible to guarantee success with any template for solutions. At the same time, however, business people who are more familiar with the traditional modes of analysis found in the managerial sciences often find the design thinking method overly complex and messy. Recognizing this, practitioners have identified three key phases that characterize the design thinking process, each with corresponding practices: inspiration, ideation and prototyping, and implementation and evaluation.

Inspiration

Inspiration is where design thinkers begin. As stated earlier, design thinking starts with the real problems that people face. It uses both quantitative and qualitative tools to get a better understanding of the problem being addressed by examining the many factors and stakeholders involved, and the corresponding relationships among all these factors and stakeholders. This may employ more traditional focus group discussions or surveys, used even in regular business processes. This encourages practitioners to immerse themselves in the actual community or area of the problem in order to get an embodied on-the-ground sense of the problem's many facets.

For example, a design thinking practitioner tasked to revamp the healthcare system for a particular hospital might first immerse himself or herself in the actual experience of a patient, from ingress to egress. Data from this direct immersion in addition to all the other data from other analyses are important in the inspiration phase, as the data and experience

---

12. Liedtka et al., *Design Thinking for the Greater Good*, 6.
13. See IDEO, *Field Guide to Human Centered Design*.

gleaned will inspire ideas, and serve as resources from which the design thinking practitioner can draw important insights for the next part of the process.

Ideation and Prototyping

The second phase of the methodology is ideation and prototyping. Design thinking encourages practitioners to brainstorm as many solutions as possible without discrimination and evaluate them only after the brainstorming phase. In this ideation phase, designers begin to make sense of what they observed in the initial inspiration phase. They gather the insights taken from their data gathering and from immersing oneself in the community or context where the problem exists. Creativity and insight are key to this process, drawing from the richness of the data gathered from the initial phase.

Once there are several ideas, designers can begin to evaluate the ideas. In evaluating the most promising idea, three criteria are employed: (1) the idea must be desirable to the client for whom the design thinking process is primarily accountable to, which should address key client problems and help clients meet their goals; (2) the idea must be feasible and the organization can procure the necessary resources to execute the idea by leveraging on the organization's existing strengths and capabilities; (3) the idea must be viable or profitable for the clients' organization for the long-term. Tim Brown lists some rules on brainstorming:

1. "The best ideas emerge when the whole organizational ecosystem—not just its designers and engineers and certainly not just management—has room to experiment.
2. Those most exposed to changing externalities (new technology, shifting consumer base, strategic threats, or opportunities) are the ones best placed to respond and most motivated to do so.
3. Ideas should not be favored based on who creates them.
4. Ideas that create a buzz—excitement or energy among the group—should be favored. Indeed, ideas should gain a vocal following, however small, before being given organizational support.
5. The 'gardening' skills of senior leadership should be used to tend, prune, and harvest ideas.

6. An overarching purpose should be articulated so that the organization has a sense of direction, and innovators don't feel the need for constant supervision."[14]

Once the most promising ideas have been identified and refined, those ideas are now ready to be implemented in a small-scale test or the "prototyping stage." Initial versions of the proposed solutions are tested and monitored as prototypes. This stage allows room for experimentation and "what-if" analysis that can be used to refine the idea before finally rolling it on the larger scale. Prototyping allows for quicker changes to be made to the idea by testing multiple ideas at the same time, generating useful feedback, and refining ideas further. The results from the experimentation at the prototyping stage provide information on the ideas' strengths and weaknesses in a real-world setting, even if it is controlled. This context provides data to infer the ideas' resulting value and if there are enough resources to pursue and refine the idea further.

Implementation and Evaluation

The last phase of design thinking is implementation and evaluating. The prototyped idea is now fully executed, and the design thinking practitioners observe the outcomes and take note of feedback from clients and stakeholders. Practitioners verify whether the intended consequences were achieved, observing also how they occurred. The practitioners also identify any unintended consequences and side effects and begin to consider possible ways to mitigate unwanted consequences or shore up unintended but positive consequences.

For example, a manufacturing project that was implemented by a business in order to save costs may also have the unintended and unforeseen consequence of minimizing usage of a toxic material. This material would have ended up in a landfill and possibly poisoned the water table. This business might, in their next iteration innovating their product, take this outcome into consideration to continue improving on the positive environmental benefits of their manufacturing process. Similarly, if the opposite had happened (i.e., there were detrimental effects to the environment from their project), such consequences could be rectified in the next iteration.

---

14. Brown, *Change by Design*, 79–80.

Iterative observations and evaluations can serve as inspiration and begin the entire process again.

DESIGN THINKING PRINCIPLES

There are certain principles in design thinking that encourage a particular way of thinking and approaching problems. This is the so-called "design thinking mindset" that is key to successful innovation. Five principles characterize the design thinking mindset: (1) empathy as a catalyst for insight; (2) creativity and prototyping as important ways of testing insights; (3) collaboration, participation, and interdisciplinarity; (4) a positive attitude towards conflict and change as important for addressing wicked problems; (5) failure and messiness as part of the process of conflict and change; and (6) optimism. Each are discussed below.

Empathy as a Catalyst for Insight

First, empathy is especially crucial in the first step (i.e., phase) of design thinking because it is necessary in properly beginning the process of data-gathering that leads to insight. It can be defined as "the effort to see the world through the eyes of others, understand the world through their experiences, and feel the world through their emotions." Empathy is considered the overarching attitude that marks the entire process of design thinking.[15] This is also not a selective kind of empathy, but rather one that can empathize with various people. "Steeping ourselves in other peoples' stories, *particularly* stories that demonstrate the complex and full humanity of people who have been vulnerable to prejudice and injustice, literally rewires our brains" and helps counter selective forms of empathy.[16]

This is especially critical in the initial identification of the problem and its characteristics. IDEO CEO Tim Brown stresses that empathy that is manifested through keen observation, shared immersion in the relevant experiences, and genuine encounters with people affected by the problem, helps design thinking practitioners to enable people to articulate genuine needs they may not have explicitly thought about or considered.[17] Design

---

15. IDEO, *Field Guide to Human Centered Design*, 56.
16. Wallace, "Empathy Is Both Better and Worse Than We Think," para. 12.
17. Brown, *Change by Design*, 50.

thinking dictates that articulating genuine needs is crucial, as these are what businesses should be responding to, instead of generating artificial needs. Brown illustrates this with the example of Zyliss, a Swiss kitchen tools company. Design thinking practitioners were able to create better kitchen tools because they took notice of the shortcuts and idiosyncrasies used by professionals in the restaurant industry. They suggested improvements to their products tailor-fitted to match the real behavior of the chefs. The chefs themselves had not explicitly articulated nor even thought about these concerns, since they arose from the adaptations and adjustments they had already learned to make. Through empathetic observation and participation, design thinking practitioners were able to come to insight as to what the clients genuinely needed, even when the clients themselves had masked over those needs or were unconscious of them.[18]

Design thinkers, like Brown, further define empathy as an attitude and habit of putting people and their needs first. Putting people first means being attentive to, understanding, and responding to people in ways that genuinely serve their well-being. To do this, design thinking practitioners must cultivate a deep understanding of the particular community they are serving by putting themselves into those people's shoes and grasping things from their perspective. They must make human connections with those they seek to serve, rather than thinking of them as guinea pigs or statistics: "it's not a matter of 'us versus them' or even 'us on behalf of them'.... [I]t has to be 'us *with* them.'"[19]

Design thinking thus cultivates empathy as a mentality for envisaging the functionality of a product or service. It is based not only on what people say or cognitively think about an issue but also what people do (i.e., their behavioral processes) and what they feel and what motivates them (i.e., the emotional or affective processes). Practitioners have to pay attention to both the people involved and to their concerns, which may be explicitly expressed or not.

To understand empathy is to value the importance of a holistic understanding of the human person, as well as the value of the community the individuals are embedded in and relate with each other. Design thinking assumes that "the whole is greater than the sum of its parts" and that the relationships and network of interactions among individuals can create

---

18. Brown, *Change by Design*, 50.
19. Brown, *Change by Design*, 55–56, 63.

"group effects" that are important to consider when trying to come up with solutions.[20]

In the end, design thinking practitioners hope that "transformative empathy," as Ashlea Powell puts it, will lead to more consideration of other viewpoints. This will lead to new and better ideas and insights for changing systems and structures that are not working for the best interest of all.[21]

Collaboration, Participation, and Interdisciplinarity

Second, collaboration in design thinking and empathy, participation, and interdisciplinarity all play important roles. Collaboration, in this particular business context, encourages businesses to see clients, workers, and consumers as "active participant[s] in the process of creation."[22] Consumers are not objects to be exploited and pushed to buy particular products or workers as simply cogs in the machine that produces goods and services. This inclusive vision of collaboration takes into account all stakeholders who are affected by the problem being addressed as well as all those who will be engaged in addressing it. In an organization, collaboration might entail creating active partnerships with clients as well as representative employees from all the departments involved in the process and even local communities who may be affected.

Participation is a crucial element of collaboration because various stakeholders contribute ideas or information to enhance the efforts of addressing the problem at hand. Upholding the principle of participation of all stakeholders requires taking seriously the concerns raised that organization leaders may not have previously recognized, especially during the implementation and evaluation phases of the design thinking process.

One of the more controversial issues pertaining to ensuring the participation of all stakeholders concerns the "participation" of the environment. There is a longstanding debate among business people and business ethicists on the status of the environment as a stakeholder. This includes how much importance and concern should be given to the environment as various forms of business decision-making takes place. There are many complexities here, including, for example, the fact that the environment does not have voice or agency in the same way a human being does. It

20. Brown, *Change by Design*, 61–62.
21. Powell, "How IDEO Designers Persuade Companies to Accept Change."
22. Brown, *Change by Design*, 65.

can be contentious when deciding as to who has the "right" to speak on behalf of the environment.[23] The perceived importance of the environment as stakeholder depends heavily on the importance ascribed by the design thinker practitioners themselves.

There is one more role connected to participation, and it is design thinking's advocacy for interdisciplinarity. This role is the integration of the information, concepts, perspectives, and methods from two or more disciplines to advance knowledge or solve a particular problem whose scope and required solutions and input is beyond one discipline alone.[24] Along with pushing for participation and asking that all stakeholders be accounted for and heard, design thinking practitioners recommend that those included in the problem-solving process come from varied disciplines. This will foster more holistic collaboration that arrives at more feasible and impactful solutions.[25] Interdisciplinarity helps practitioners avoid the phenomenon of groupthink, where everyone simply agrees on one thing, and an opinion initially expressed by one party contaminates or unduly influences subsequently expressed opinions. Design thinking practitioners aim to create a space where a variety of ideas may arise. More ideas mean more chances of finding those that will most effectively respond to the wicked problem. This focus on interdisciplinarity opens the doors to dialogue with Catholic social thought and invites ethicists and theologians in the field of Catholic social thought to enter into this dialogue.

Creativity and Prototyping as Important Ways of Testing Insights

One of the central principles of design thinking is the importance of creativity and out-of-the-box thinking in crafting solutions. Design thinking itself as a methodology was conceived as a way to help people become more creative problem-solvers. IDEO speaks of cultivating "creative confidence," to empower people to conceive of and play with fresh, even wild, ideas and then test them on smaller scales. In many cases, the prototyping process has revealed that seemingly "wild" ideas were the solutions needed for

---

23. See Haigh and Griffiths, "Natural Environment as Primary Stakeholder," 347–59; Starik, "Should Trees Have Managerial Standing?," 207–17; Jacobs, "Environment as Stakeholder," 25–28; Woodward, "Is the Natural Environment a Stakeholder?"

24. See Aldrich, *Interdisciplinarity*.

25. See Currie et al., "Call for University-Based Business Schools to 'Lower Their Walls,'" 742–55.

successful innovation.[26] Through prototyping, design thinking practitioners learn how people interact with the possible solution in a lower risk setting. By offering a space for such creativity, prototyping allows wilder ideas that may at first seem unfeasible or not viable to be refined.

Positive Attitude Towards Conflict and Change as Important for Addressing Wicked Problems

Fourth, a positive attitude towards conflict and change is a hallmark of design thinking. Because design thinking is convinced that the systems in place can be changed, certain changes can bring about progress that mitigates a wicked problem. Undergirding the entire design thinking enterprise is thus a sense of optimism or even hope:

> Design is inherently optimistic. . . . Optimism is the embrace of possibility, the idea that even if we don't know the answer, . . . we can find it. . . . Optimism makes us more creative, encourages us to push on . . . [and] infuses the entire process with the energy and drive . . . to navigate the thorniest problems.[27]

While design thinking acknowledges the many constraints, variables, and conflicting goods and needs involved in "large and intractable problems" like poverty, climate change, or economic inequality, practitioners still "have to believe that progress is . . . an option. If we didn't, we wouldn't even try."[28] Problems can indeed be solved, or at least partially worked on to achieve particular goals set by the design thinking practitioners. Design thinking is recommended as a method that can contribute to practical strategies for advancing the common good so that better living conditions for all can be had.

The optimism of the design thinking process, however, does not imply that all ideas should be treated positively, or that everyone should be encouraged to implement every idea regardless of its feasibility, viability, or desirability. However, it does call practitioners to regularly hear out ideas fairly and help people refine the ideas to become better, rather than cynically killing new ideas without first understanding them and the contexts from which they emerge.

26. IDEO, *Field Guide to Human Centered Design*, 19.
27. IDEO, *Field Guide to Human Centered Design*, 24.
28. IDEO, *Field Guide to Human Centered Design*, 24.

The complexities that arise from wicked problems—including the many iterations necessitated to solve them sufficiently—also demand that the design thinking practitioner be comfortable with change and manage and adapt to changes as they happen. Because they are willing to implement more creative and unorthodox solutions, conflict may arise due to the clashing of opinions, perspectives, expertise, risk appetites. Because there are many stakeholders involved in the process of addressing a wicked problem, there will always be many goods and needs to weigh and consider. Given the reality of limited resources and the inevitable prioritization of certain goods over others, conflict is inevitably going to be present. Being willing to engage in conflict in a healthy way as well as be willing to adapt to and bring about change is required in the design thinking process.

Design thinking practitioners do not shy away from conflict. Constructive conflict is seen as an important part of the solution-generating process. While careful to ensure that these conflicts do not devolve into meaningless fighting or arguments, the design thinking methodology allow for debates and disagreements to happen, without necessarily looking for an end goal of total harmony or complete consensus. Rather than seeking absolute harmony, design thinking practitioners might look for fair and just compromises and encourage a facilitated debate or process that balances in the fairest manner the short-term versus the long-term. Empathy enters the frame once again to facilitate charitable listening to respectful airing of different positions, create a more conducive environment for compromise, collaboration, and find equitable ways forward, even on difficult and potentially polarizing issues.

At times, the process of change itself gives rise to increased conflict. Certain intended changes may be unwanted by particular groups of people, or because unintended consequences occur, elicit disparate evaluations and responses from the different stakeholders. Through empathy, design thinkers hope to shift people's perspectives in the face of conflict: "the desired outcome is that stakeholders come away from the experience in agreement about the challenge we are solving and with a felt understanding of why things need to change."[29] In the face of conflict, design thinking practitioners are willing to confront the situation where the conflict arose and facilitate conversations or activities to create plans to resolve the conflict. Through careful crafting and implementation of the dialogue and the

---

29. Powell, "How IDEO Designers Persuade Companies to Accept Change," para. 3.

projects themselves, as well as the willingness to compromise, design thinkers believe many conflicts can be alleviated.

Failure and Messiness as Part of the Process of Conflict and Change

Fifth, design thinking's creative process entails testing solutions early through prototyping, especially in the face of testing new and creative ideas to find a solution in the face of the various conflicts that may arise in the process. Practitioners can manage risk while expeditiously putting innovative ideas into practice: "when the goal is to get impactful solutions out into the world, you can't live in abstractions, you have to make them real."[30]

As stated earlier, design thinkers do not expect to get it all right immediately on the first attempt. Failure and messiness are part of the process, and design thinking practitioners understand that there will be times that they will need to go back to ideating, prototyping, or even brainstorming. Any solution for a wicked problem attempted will be, in many ways, a "one shot operation." It is non-replicable, as the attempt itself would have direct influence on the conditions and constraints of the already complicated and indeterminate wicked problem.

Rather than a once-and-for-all approach to responding to a problem, therefore, design thinkers focus on how to improve by employing a series of solutions or responses. Through iteration, or continuous responses to a problem, where the outcome of each response becomes the starting point of the next response, design thinkers "validate . . . ideas along the way because we're hearing from the people we're actually designing for"[31] and, more broadly, receiving feedback by observing their action's intended and unintended effects and consequences. Iteration entails not just executing solutions, but also eliciting feedback to evaluate the solution and its created enactment. This will craft a new response and iteration capable of bringing the community a step closer to solving the wicked problem, rather than reinforcing the status quo or even making the problem worse.

Victor Papanek illustrates the value of this iterative approach using the example of the creation of the car at the turn of the twentieth century in the United States. The car had been invented as a solution to the problem of transport and access. However, it was impossible to predict the exact impact of the car. "No one foresaw that mass acceptance of the car would

---

30. IDEO, *Field Guide to Human Centered Design*, 20.
31. IDEO, *Field Guide to Human Centered Design*, 25.

put the American bedroom on wheels, offering everyone a new place to copulate. . . . [N]obody expected the car to accelerate our mobility, thereby creating the exurban sprawl and the dormitory suburbs that strangle our larger cities . . . or to dislocate our societal groupings, thus contributing to our alienation."[32] Every succeeding generation of the car has continuously adapted to address the new situations that arise with the previous generation. Similar things may be said about how certain products or inventions have disrupted business, such as the way the internet and online shopping have disrupted the traditional brick-and-mortar retail shops.

Inevitably, not all pertinent information is readily available or easily identified. As a result, overlooked aspects of the problem endure, or possibly even worsen, after a solution is implemented. Practitioners may thus find themselves with a solution that, while initially effective, no longer works, hence the need to continue brainstorming, ideating, and prototyping.

On the one hand, design thinking allows a degree of comfort with failure in its process, given the constraints mentioned above. This is the purpose of the prototyping stage, where design thinking practitioners can "fail early" on a smaller scale. This is important because too much risk aversion can lead to missed opportunities for positive change. On the other hand, though, design thinking also cautions practitioners to take failures seriously, as these would have real-world effects.

The iterative process gives deliberate space for failure, but it is not an invitation to recklessness. The process must be carried out with great concern for the stakeholders. Design thinking practitioners must not operate as if everything were trial and error with no consequences. They need to think through and evaluate each iteration with care: asking what happened during the implementation, who and what were affected for good or ill, and what steps to take next given both the consequences of the iteration and the feedback received.

CRITIQUES OF DESIGN THINKING

Design thinking is not without its limitations and critics, and there are two main critiques against this methodology. Both have to do with the way power and social location operate in the design thinking process.

First, practitioners of design thinking have been accused of failing to ensure a genuine inclusive participation of all stakeholders. Despite stated

32. Papanek, *Design for the Real World*, 10.

intentions, Natasha Iskander, associate professor of Urban Planning and Public Service at New York University, points out that design thinking in actual practice inevitably "privileges the designer above the people she serves, and in doing so, limits participation in the design process and limits the scope for truly innovative ideas."[33] All the power to define the parameters of the problem—along with the parameters for possible solutions—lies in the hands of the group of people directing the design thinking process.

Thus, the vision and goal of the process are heavily dictated by the members of the directing group, the members with the greatest influence and loudest voice within that group, and the group's leaders. While it might be true in certain cases that simply following the dictates of the powerful few who can make quick decisions can result in clearer, more productive, and more efficient implementation of projects, the results will more likely be for profit and for the benefit of the powerful, rather than for the larger common good.

By favoring the viewpoints of the more powerful, who have a vested interest in the status quo, this positional bias, in particular, "makes it hard to solve challenges that are characterized by a high degree of uncertainty—like climate change—where doing things the way we always have done them is a sure recipe for disaster." Too often, the prototyped and implemented solutions are not the best but rather those that are favored by those in power or by the majority. Even the highly valued practice of empathy can be distorted. Iskander explains that "because the designer herself generates the tacit understandings she uses by connecting empathetically with potential users—the 'empathize' mode—whatever needs of product users and communities she perceives are refracted through her personal experience and priorities."[34] Design thinking often does not pay attention to this positionality or its implications.[35]

A second and related critique of the design thinking methodology is its lack of any definite social vision or transformational goal. When left unarticulated, the overarching social vision of the project is left in the hands of the designers—whether implicitly or explicitly. Central to the design thinking process is the shared vision that brings the various stakeholders together and keeps the group on track. Often, however, this shared vision is something crafted and articulated by the designers only or those at the

---

33. Iskander, "Design Thinking," par. 3.
34. Iskander, "Design Thinking," par. 3.
35. Iskander, "Design Thinking," par. 11.

top of the organization with no involvement by the other stakeholders. The orienting vision now becomes heavily dependent on the composition and power dynamics of the group, where only a small minority benefits from the overall process at the expense of the rest of the stakeholders and wider society. For example, on paper, the stipulated vision or goal of a project might be the aim of improving living conditions by way of a process that attempts to balance feasibility, profitability or viability, and desirability. In practice, however, profitability or viability often become the more important criteria, as these are the metrics familiar to many businesses. Stakeholder desirability and long-term feasibility that benefit more people are often subordinated.

Jussi Pasanen, an expert in design thinking and human-centered design, adds another level to this critique, and approaches it from an environmental perspective. He contends that design both suffers from and itself fosters extreme anthropocentrism while also arguing that the disruptive innovations that design thinking produces actually leads to harm for certain groups. He gives the example of AirBnb, a vacation rental online marketplace that eliminates big corporate middlemen and allows virtually anyone to join and profit from the bed-and-breakfast industry. Often hailed as a game-changing innovator: "Airbnb helps you '*find adventures nearby or in faraway places and access unique homes, experiences, and places around the world.*' The end-to-end experience is crafted, seamless and highly polished for the traveler and the host alike. However, Airbnb also skews housing affordability in many cities. It facilitates mass tourism with many negative impacts on local communities."[36] Similarly, he argues, Uber, the acclaimed ride-sharing app that disrupted both the car rental and taxi industries, provides great ease to commuters but also came with many negative effects:

> Uber is a "*ridesharing app for fast, reliable rides in minutes.*" Again, the experience is super convenient and very slick. . . . At first glance, their service may appear like a marketplace, however it most certainly is not a real or a level one. Uber forces traditional taxi operators out of business, impacts drivers' livelihoods, and increases traffic congestion in cities like New York.[37]

This kind of analysis, Pasanen believes, must force businesses to reconsider who truly benefits from the operations, and who are ignored, left out, and hurt by the design thinking process. Pasanen concludes, "not all

---

36. Pasanen, "Human Centred Design Considered Harmful," par. 15.
37. Pasanen, "Human Centred Design Considered Harmful," par. 16, 18.

humans are equal in the typical human-centered design process" because those in power or those at the head of the design thinking process tend to have a greater voice.[38] There is still the tendency to favor profitability over anything else. In these circumstances, the overriding questions of the design thinking process overlook the good of all stakeholders in favor of whatever would "increase revenue, decrease costs, increase new market share, increase revenue from existing customers, increase shareholder value . . . [in other words], does it make money? Does it save money? Does it reduce [financial] risk?"[39]

Design thinking, when packaged into a "neat" process that disproportionately focuses only on one particular group of more powerful stakeholders, will not lead to the innovation and inclusive change for the stakeholders that design thinking promotes. Employing this method may even contribute to harming certain groups and, as the examples show, this is what many design-thinking oriented organizations and businesses have in fact done. Under these circumstances, design thinking, rather than innovating and responding effectively to wicked problems, ends up prioritizing the interests of those in power and preserving the status quo for them.

THE VALUE OF DIALOGUE BETWEEN DESIGN THINKING AND THEOLOGY AS METHOD FOR DISRUPTION

In the discipline of theology, a number of scholars and practitioners have brought aspects and concepts from design thinking into conversation with missiology, spirituality, and theological ethics, but they have not fully developed the connections. For example, scholar Willis Jenkins at the University of Virginia describes the complex issue of climate change with wicked problems. Jenkins describes his project as part of a theocentric and prophetic pragmatism, that "the struggle to invent practical responses to overwhelming social problems is a struggle to give faithful answer to God for the world and so should be understood as a proper theological exercise."[40] Beyond the shared worldview that religious traditions provide, Jenkins's theocentric and prophetic pragmatism "supposes that its most important resources are the tactics generated by communities using their traditions to confront new problems;" such tactics, he contends, "cultivate opportunities

38. Pasanen, "Human Centred Design Considered Harmful," par. 19.
39. Pasanen, "Human Centred Design Considered Harmful."
40. Jenkins, *Future of Ethics*, 69.

for moral agency to bear responsibility for unprecedented problems, and thereby permit moral agents to sustain the meaning of life carried by their tradition of faith."[41]

In response to environmental crises, sustainability science is not just an abstract endeavor but includes the cooperative tasks of both solving problems and changing deep-seated contexts. Jenkins brings in the concept of wicked problems as part of sustainability science's method of managing problems by including, rather than excluding, religion and cultures. Because, for Jenkins, transforming cultures is a task that religious communities often foster. It makes sense to bring religious communities' thought and cultures into conversation with wicked problems.[42] In framing issues of sustainability and environmental degradation as enormously complex and in many ways unprecedented wicked problems, theocentric pragmatists' strategies should "depend on culture-transforming creativity," generated from within their own particular cultures; Jenkins defines this as containing a "'tool kit' of symbols, stories, rituals, and world views which people may use in varying configurations to solve different kinds of problems."[43] By drawing on the tool kit of religious culture, particularly the tools of prophetic questioning offered by various religious traditions, prophetic pragmatists can assist sustainability scientists in reflecting on the appropriate goals and solutions for their projects and help motivate people to pursue them.

Writing from the field of Christian business ethics, Michael Hodson, former head of the social enterprise incubator at Regent College in Vancouver, proposes that design thinking might be the "missing link" between theology and business practice.[44] He emphasizes New Testament scholar N. T. Wright's theological vision, which focuses on developing virtue and flourishing using reflection on Christian Scripture. For Hodson, design thinking offers a method where businesspeople can recognize the contributions theology can make in the realm of business, which can then be used to brainstorm how these contributions might be used to help improve the

---

41. Jenkins, *Future of Ethics*, 81.

42. Jenkins, *Future of Ethics*, 150, 156.

43. Jenkins, *Future of Ethics*, 172.

44. A social enterprise incubator is a space that offers the tools for business people, specifically social entrepreneurs, to jumpstart and maintain their enterprise geared towards creating social good.

business's vision and mission towards the common good.[45] He stresses that "[one's] theology helps set the purpose of the design. The designer works in a way that is analogous of the way God works—with purpose."[46] Using N. T. Wright's work to bring Christian Scripture to bear on people's ethics, in dialogue with a design thinking framework, Hodson further comments that "biblical theology presents us with many examples to avoid, if we can but make the right translation into our own time. . . . Defining what the result doesn't look like nevertheless leaves much scope for designing many forms of 'solution' to the design problem."[47]

Hodson connects design thinking with theological ethics by noting the importance of ongoing evaluation in both the business world and the moral life. The repeated evaluation and iteration that are important to design thinking are also important to business practice and to theological ethics.[48] Similar to the process of spiritual discernment in determining whether or not a person is developing towards moral virtue, evaluation in business is a way that people can analyze and articulate whether or not their practices or strategies are in consonance with the organization's values and established vision.

Given the varied but potentially mutually illuminating principles, features, strengths, and weaknesses of design thinking and Catholic social thought outlined in this and the previous chapter, there is something of value to be had in bringing design thinking and theology together through Catholic social thought: that is, for the purpose of understanding and addressing business problems marked by great structural and moral complexity. Hodson's work identifies initial points of agreement between design thinking and various branches of theology that can be relevant for business and suggests ways that business ethics may be able to incorporate and learn from theology. Jenkins's work is also important as it articulates the importance of this kind of cross- or interdisciplinary work as a form of doing theology, and not simply a secondary step of applying theology.

Drawing on Catholic social thought to identify concepts and principles for the tool kit, Christian prophetic pragmatists can use this toolkit to respond to unprecedented problems, especially in the business arena. Secular organizations must take seriously the cultural practices of a community

45. Hodson, "Design Thinking," 23–25.
46. Hodson, "Design Thinking," 24.
47. Hodson, "Design Thinking," 24.
48. Hodson, "Design Thinking," 25.

when engaging complex social or environmental problems, such as climate change, and these practices include religious practices and theology. Organizations working to address problems like climate change can face major obstacles if their projects go against the community's culture and make it difficult for the community members to participate. Therefore, working with culture in mind helps organizations facilitate their socially transformative projects and achieve the desired results in ways that are more permanent and disruptive towards the good. The same work must be done with religious practices and theology in the same that way organizations take culture seriously. Organizations also need to take seriously the diverse ways religious categories are used to help (or hinder) the work of solving complex societal and environmental problems. This knowledge should be included in the tool kit to help respond to the unprecedented problems in business.

CONCLUSION: DESIGN THINKING AS A METHODOLOGY FOR DISRUPTION

Design thinking has been used by various businesses and organizations to innovate their operations, structures, and strategies. For business people, design thinking as a language harnesses creativity in solving the complex business problems of today. For those outside of business, design thinking is also used for social issues and creating social and environmental impact in education, healthcare, welfare, and urban planning. This method has been used to disrupt the status quo in different industries and help people generate new insights to address the issues they are facing in ways that are ethical and also consider the social and environmental aspects of an issue.

Design thinking and its understanding of and approach to wicked problems can help Catholic leaders, ethicists, and practitioners in their efforts to describe and respond to structures of sin, to disrupt the very real structures and ways of being in the world that led to injustice and other social and environmental problems. Catholic social thought understands sinful structures and, similar to design thinking, they both seek to articulate the ways in which the complex systems and structures that human beings navigate both help and harm people and the environment, by amplifying or synergizing the effects of human actions, both intended and unintended.

With respect to transforming or dismantling structures of sin, Catholic social thought, ethics, and practice can learn to address wicked problems through the "identification and connection of chains of contingencies that could shape the future. . . . [T]he purpose of an 'applied forward reasoning' approach is to identify ways in which interventions might create particular policy pathways that move toward preferred outcomes."[49] Catholic thinkers and practitioners seeking to respond to structures of sin may also benefit from other applications of design thinking.[50] Design thinking offers a methodology and specific toolkit for ethicists and theologians who are looking for ways to operationalize the concepts in Catholic social thought. Operationalizing these concepts offers ethicists and theologians experiences and further reflection that can enrich the current body of knowledge in Catholic social thought. It helps concretize the effects and implications Catholic social thought is concerned about, and further elaborated on given these effects and implications, whether intentional or unintentional. Lastly, design thinking offers a language and entrance into business that business people can understand and put into practice, help ethicists and theologians articulate a just but practical way of doing business, in response to the critique that business ethics and Catholic social thought are "utopic" or "naïve" and not a feasible practice for businesses to actually do.

At the same time, Catholic social thought can offer its own particular social vision and principles, to protect from design thinking's weaknesses, and to avoid becoming just another form of traditional disruption with more negative than positive effects. For design thinkers in business for the common good, the Catholic social thought principles and vision can help guide and keep the process on track, remind design thinking practitioners of what is at stake, as well as what is being worked towards. This is what some Catholic social thinkers describe as dismantling structures of sin and building up structures of grace. In the next chapter, we will elaborate upon the ways that dialogue between the two disciplines can be deepened for disruption in business.

---

49. Levin et al., "Overcoming the Tragedy of Super Wicked Problems," 131.
50. See Kolawole, "Design for Worldview."

CHAPTER 4

Design Thinking and Catholic Social Thought: A Dialogue for Disruption

AT THIS POINT, WE have explored the strengths and contributions, as well as the weaknesses and criticisms of both design thinking and Catholic social thought in their dialogue with business ethics. Catholic social thought offers vision and principles for a community where all creation flourishes. On their own, however, these vision and principles are inadequate for addressing the specific nuances of business ethics. Further development is required in grappling with the systemic aspects of sin in business. Because not everybody shares the same religious background or understands what Catholic social thought assumes or says due to its religious nature, Catholic social ethicists require resources and tools to engage in the pluralistic setting of business ethics, as well as respond to the critique of being too ideal to the point of impracticality. Design thinking offers a concrete methodology that encourages creativity and systems thinking in crafting solutions to unprecedented and complex problems. However, these often lack, in actual practice, genuine participation and a greater vision for society. This is something Catholic social thought can help make more robust through the reflection of theologians and ethicists on solidarity, subsidiarity, and the common good.

To advance this dialogue, three points of intersection between these fields of thought and practice first need to be identified: (1) empathy and human-centeredness; (2) optimism versus hope; and (3) understanding the role of conflict and risk. We will then identify specific contributions of design thinking to Catholic social thought and vice versa emerging from the points of intersection and divergence. This will be helpful to businesses to navigate ethical issues—especially those of a systemic nature—related to their organization and work's activities towards disruption.

POINTS OF DIALOGUE

Empathy and Human-Centeredness

The first point of common ground between Catholic social thought and design thinking is empathy and human-centeredness. This especially pertains to the step of "seeing" in the Catholic see-judge-act paradigm, and to "inspiration" in design thinking. Empathy is also key in disruption because it requires an attentiveness to any and all kinds of businesses opportunities as well as to particular kinds of opportunities and alternatives that can reshape the way business is done towards improvement and transformation for the better. Describing and fleshing out the foundations as well of this empathy and human-centeredness grounds the transformation being aimed for in a vision of a life-giving and just society.

In the discussion on design thinking, empathy is an important cornerstone for its process. Empathy assumes human-centeredness, and design thinking practitioners must put themselves into the shoes of the people that they are designing for to gain a better grasp of the problem and its solutions. This approach is not about staying in the office reading and analyzing issues but rather actually going out and doing forms of fieldwork, immersing oneself in the world and in the issue that is being addressed. Doing so allows the design thinking practitioner to experience what others are experiencing and to grasp, even if not in its totality, what a particular community is going through in a particular situation.

In Catholic social thought, human-centeredness, and empathy, when rightly understood in connection with God and the environment, form part of the foundation for the practice of solidarity—especially solidarity with the poor and the marginalized. The ability to empathize through acknowledging the connection between interpersonal relationships and the common good is an important condition for being in solidarity with others. Meghan Clark describes how solidarity is "almost a synonym for interdependence" and an "ethical imperative" for communities to "live and act in particular ways"—ways that are consistent with a commitment towards the common good and integral human development.[1] Francis also highlights

---

1. Clark, *Vision of Catholic Social Thought*, 19–21.

empathy and solidarity when rejecting the bubbles of indifference that people have become used to living in, which makes them "insensitive to the cries of the people."[2]

When justifying the importance of solidarity as a principle in Catholic social thought, the norm of human-centeredness arises from the intrinsic value and dignity of human beings, due to their being created in the "image and likeness" of God. This latter phrase can mean many things. Theologians have sought to describe the *imago Dei* by pointing out the unique and life-giving characteristics human beings possess, including the ability to reason and reflect on our relationality and participation in God's creative actions.[3] At the Second Vatican Council, "invoking the theme of the image of God, the Council affirmed in *Gaudium et Spes* the dignity of man . . . [which] consists in man's fundamental orientation to God, which is the basis of human dignity and of the inalienable rights of the human person."[4] The council describes this in trinitarian terms and explains how Jesus Christ "restores the divine likeness" that was lost through sin.[5] They continue to note that "on the basis of the doctrine of the image of God, the Council teaches that human activity reflects the divine creativity which is its model and must be directed to justice and human fellowship in order to foster the establishment of one family in which all are brothers and sisters."[6]

This intrinsic value of human beings is the foundation of solidarity. Solidarity entails recognizing and taking responsibility for the fact of human interconnection in an unwavering commitment to the common good, that is, to attend to both the individual good and the good of the community because they are connected. In the Catholic social understanding of the common good, the well-being of the individual human person is not separate from the well-being of the community.

However, this does not mean that any one person or group of persons can be forced to shoulder majority of societal burdens for the good of the community. The individual rights that flow from the same God-given dignity must be upheld for everyone. Thus, solidarity sees every human being as an important and valuable member of the community. This means giving

---

2. Francis, "Homily of Holy Father Francis," para. 6.

3. See Grenz, *Social God and the Relational Self*; Haslam, *Constructive Theology of Intellectual Disability*; Berry, "What Makes Us Human?," 87–106.

4. International Theological Commission, "Communion and Stewardship," sec. 22.

5. International Theological Commission, "Communion and Stewardship," sec. 22.

6. International Theological Commission, "Communion and Stewardship," sec. 22.

the needs, concerns, contributions, and lives of each and every human being precedence over the wants of the few in power.

While empathy and human-centeredness are important in design thinking and Catholic social thought, both disciplines have acknowledged that human-centeredness should not come at the expense of the well-being of the environment. This is a key development especially when it comes to disrupting economic and business systems, given the rising concern for climate change and environmental degradation. Human-centeredness is at risk of becoming destructive anthropocentrism if it is brought to its extreme.

However, current literature on the environment and the ecological crisis has enabled both design thinking and Catholic social thought to be more ecologically conscious. Pope Francis, for example, has made ecological concern a central pillar of his papacy. This comes alongside increasing concern with sustainability in the realm of business ethics as well as for businesses to pay more attention to the impact of human action on the environment and call for a rethinking of the principle of human-centeredness. Human-centeredness is an important principle for both disciplines, but environmental concerns are also an equally important consideration.[7]

Design thinking encourages interdisciplinarity and the consultation of all stakeholders in the problem-solving process, grounded in this empathy. For design thinking practitioners, interdisciplinarity goes beyond simple multidisciplinarity because it is intentionally integrative:

> [In] multidisciplinarity (disciplinary courses that are informed by other disciplines)—the disciplinary contributions may be mutual and cumulative but they are not considered integrated. . . . Synthetic interdisciplinarity [on the other hand] occurs when teaching issues and research questions bridge disciplines. These bridging issues and questions are of two subtypes: (1) issues or questions that are found in the intersections of disciplines, and (2) issues and questions that are found in the gaps between disciplines.[8]

Interdisciplinarity, as it is understood, requires rigor and care. The practitioner needs to be familiar with the material involved in each field when crossing disciplines. Interdisciplinarity also entails articulating a clear set of goals and expectations, as well as self-reflection questions. These

---

7. See Bauckham, *Bible and Ecology*; Johnson, *Ask the Beasts*; Nash, *Loving Nature*; Living Climate Change, "All about Climate Change."

8. Sapiro, "Interdisciplinary and Collaborative Teaching," 12.

questions include how sources from other disciplines are incorporated, how sources are chosen, the advantage of choosing certain sources over others, and more specific questions like "to what extent can we escape our own culture or disciplinary perspective," and "are there any borders that cannot or should not be crossed?"[9]

Catholic social thought's espousal of the principle of subsidiarity promotes a more decentralized way of making decisions. In particular, its way includes the voices of those who are most affected by the issue at hand and the voices of those outside the centers of power who are often not heard. This principle is also grounded in the idea of human dignity, with each person's dignity making them equally valuable and worthy of being heard. The principle of subsidiarity, however, also acknowledges that there are occasions when keeping the decisions and solutions to the most local levels is insufficient. There are certain decisions and solutions that need the resources and synergy that larger institutions offer, as well as the specialized expertise of professionals in their various fields. International organizations and experts, for example, would be able to do many things that local government units or civil organizations may not be able to do due to access to resources or scale.

The principle of subsidiarity resists, however, the extreme version of the previous idea; that is, a way of organizing and mobilizing resources that does not heed what is happening on the ground, and treats certain human beings as more important, thus having more privilege and right to be heard compared to others. Rather than extremely centralizing power and decision-making in the hands of a few, this principle calls for broadly identifying stakeholders and ensuring appropriate participation in the process to those identified, even within the hierarchical organizational design of business. However, in practice, as shown in the previous chapter, this priority for participation is easier to write into the mission statements of organizations than it is to concretely follow through on in actual decision-making.

The principle of subsidiarity has also been used in the realm of business, and is most often understood as stakeholder empowerment, engagement, and participation. This, however, becomes a catchphrase that is often employed but insufficiently practiced. Even in employing design thinking, there is a tendency for organizations to still prioritize profit and financial returns over equitable participation of all stakeholders in decision-making. Typically, the voices of those in power or at the top of

---

9. Sapiro, "Interdisciplinary and Collaborative Teaching," 17.

the management—because of their clout, finances, or vested interests—are given the most weight. Profit is also often the primary focus, due to its being seen as the chief indicator of business success and the most significant resource to keep the business concern going. While many businesses speak of the importance of people, customers, and the environment, at the end of the day, many of these same companies still treat financial indicators, including net profit value or return on investment, as the end goal and primary criterion for decision-making. This focus on profit more than anything else explains the seeming paradox of companies that launch numerous sustainability projects or initiatives to care for local communities while simultaneously engaging in business operations that primarily do the opposite.

One such case is the multinational company Nestlé, a food and drink processing conglomerate with operations all over the world. Nestlé prides itself in its "Creating Shared Value" business strategy which emphasizes the mutual benefits that both their business and society should receive from their operations. One example is Nestlé removing middlemen from their transactions with coffee farmers, such as those in the Philippines. They source directly from the farmers in order to give them higher compensation, instead of going through middlemen who take a cut of the profit from the farmers. This results in lower costs for Nestlé coffee.[10]

Despite this strategy, however, Nestlé also has projects that harm local communities and the environment, like their bottled water production in Canada in the early 2000s. Nestlé's operations continued to extract water out of ground wells even amid the droughts—severely affecting the local communities' water supply. In 2005, Nestlé CEO Peter Brabeck was quoted as saying that "water should not be considered a human right and be instead treated as a 'foodstuff commodity'"—this is evidenced in the case of Hillsburgh, Ontario, an area that had suffered at least three major drought events since 2007. Nestlé's operations extracted 1.1 million liters of water daily and continued to do so even in the midst of the droughts. Public pressure eventually caused the provincial government to intervene and restrict the daily extraction of water—however Nestlé lobbied back and eventually the restrictions were overturned.[11]

Even within the Catholic church, where subsidiarity is a principle that has been developed in Catholic social thought since *Quadragesimo Anno* in

10. See Nestlé, "Nestlé Supports Coffee."
11. See Subramaniam, "Look into Nestlé's Controversial Water Bottling Business."

1931. Local church hierarchies and organizations have struggled to communicate and implement the principle. There has been debate on whether or not subsidiarity or more democratic forms of organizational hierarchy should be applied to the church.[12]

For example, Leonardo Legazpi points out that during the Second Plenary Council of the Philippines (PCP II) in 1991 there was a "blunting of the concrete empirical surveys" that had been "painstakingly done" before the council in order to learn more about the lights and shadows of issues facing Filipinos. This resulted in the lessening of the voices of the lay and the marginalized in the council's process.[13] Another example is criticisms leveled against the recent synod on the family in 2015, which was meant to collate reflections on the various issues surrounding the family from the lay members of basic ecclesial communities and various dioceses from all over the world. In the Philippines, the survey that was given contained leading questions that prompted a particular response. Thus, the data collected was not very accurate in terms of gauging the concerns of lay Filipino Catholics. The proceedings of the synod formed the foundation for the apostolic exhortation *Amoris Laetitia*, a document that tackled the day-to-day realities of families and married couples and how the Catholic church might accompany people through those realities. The questions raised pertained as to why, for instance, women were not allowed to vote in the synod on the family—where women's voices were especially crucial given the subject matter.[14] What happened at the synod on the family also reflected the experiences of the women at the Second Vatican Council fifty years earlier, where women were invited but had no direct input.[15] Today, some women theologians continue to raise concerns about how open the Catholic church is to the participation of women and other marginalized groups.[16]

There are, however, many positive developments and hopeful signs of positive change towards genuine subsidiarity under Francis's papacy. Francis has called multiple times for the expansion of women's leadership in the Catholic church at the same time, emphasizing the importance of the laity's participation. However, several theologians have critiqued this call as lacking and still supports a more essentialist way of understanding

---

12. Pius XI, *Quadragesimo Anno*, sec. 80; see Nichols, *That All May Be One*; Hamrlik, "Principle of Subsidiarity and Catholic Ecclesiology."

13. Legaspi, "Looking Back, Looking Forward," 4.

14. Martin, "*Where Were the Voting Women at the Synod?*"

15. McEnroy, *Guests in Their Own House*.

16. See Sanchez, "Where Is Women's Wisdom in the Life of the Church?," 27–43.

men and women.[17] For example, in his 2020 post-synodal exhortation *Querida Amazonia*, Francis still emphasizes the "proper" places for women to contribute, in response to the question of women's ordination.[18] Francis's papacy is also marked by a movement towards more collegiality with his fellow bishops, as well as dialogue with other churches and religions, with governments, and with other organizations in order to foster the common good.[19]

Optimism and Hope

The second point for dialogue involves the related ideas of optimism and hope. While design thinking and Catholic social thought share a positive view of what can be done for a more just future, the choices of terms to describe this positive posture disclose some significant differences. Design thinking encourages an attitude of "optimism" when trying to generate solutions for wicked problems, where positive changes are applied to the current way of doing things. The current way doesn't need to stay that way and effort and resources should be placed into imagining and enacting a way forward, which also supports the work of ethical disruption.

Design thinking is future-oriented, concerned with imagining the possibilities and enacting concrete changes. Through the prototyping process in particular, these changes are iterated in a manner that allows design thinking practitioners to "fail early in order to succeed earlier" in their quest for results. Even when faced with obstacles, roadblocks, and detours along the process, design thinking advocates maintain that change is still possible and can be achieved by going through the design thinking methodology. Even failure and false starts are viewed as a positive because they are necessary on the path towards concrete positive change, despite being unconventional—according to traditional business analysts' logic.

Catholic social thought, for its part, is underpinned by the virtue of hope, which is arguably similar to design thinking's optimism. The human virtue of hope encourages the possibility of change and progress, but it does not rely solely on empirical logic or methods to move towards that change.

---

17. While there are diverse ways of understanding sexuality and other aspects of social-embodied reality, I use these examples to illustrate the complexity and connections between social teaching and other aspects of moral theology ethics such as sexual teaching in Catholicism.

18. Francis, "Dicastery for the Laity, the Family, and Life," sec. 101.

19. Francis, *Laudato Si'*, sec. 14, 40–50.

People motivated by specifically Christian hope have a further theologically-grounded faith that, while there may be successes and defeats, God will, overall, ensure that, in the end—albeit not always in the present or short run—good will triumph. Theologian Jürgen Moltmann describes Christian hope as the orientation of "present-day justice and reconciliation efforts to the final transformation of creation made possible through the resurrection."[20] People motivated by such hope are oriented towards the future as graced by God, while remaining rooted in the present and the past. For Christians, this hope is not individualistic but rather social and they hope for a communal salvation rather than a solely individualistic one.[21] "While this community-oriented vision of the 'blessed life' is certainly directed beyond the present world," writes Benedict XVI, "it also has to do with the building up of this world—in very different ways, according to the historical context and the possibilities offered or excluded thereby."[22] Hope, so understood, is not a strategy, like how optimism is popularly understood to be in the business world.[23] Rather, Christian hope rallies present action towards a particular vision of well-being, often called *shalom*—which is peace, right relations, and flourishing of humanity and all creation—in short, what ethical disruption also moves towards.[24]

These insights on Christian hope and optimism can be related to the iterative aspect of design thinking in generating solutions. On the one hand, both design thinking's optimism and Christian hope admit the possibility of a path to progress that is marked with leaps forward and leaps back, detours and side routes, and various difficulties. Despite these obstacles and roadblocks, however, Christian hope and design thinking maintains that change is possible and can be achieved by going through and trusting their respective processes. This is especially true for design thinking that sometimes goes against traditional established business logic, which may assume a more or less continual ascent with perhaps some corrections due to the boom-bust cycle.

Yet on the other hand, there are at least two important distinctions to be made between the optimism of design thinking and Christian hope. First, the Catholic social thought perspective warns on simply relying on technological advancement to achieve progress as well as the temptation

---

20. See Hoover-Kinsinger, *Hoping against Hope*, 313.
21. Benedict XVI, *Spe Salvi*, secs. 13–14.
22. Benedict XVI, *Spe Salvi*, sec. 15.
23. See Page, *Hope Is Not a Strategy*; Gee, *Hope Is Not a Strategy*.
24. See Birch, *What Does the Lord Require?*, 20–31.

to a reductionist understanding that equates progress with technological advances alone. Francis cautions against this "technocratic paradigm," wherein humanity assumes that all new developments automatically equate to genuine increase in well-being for creation, and that humanity will always be progressing. "There is a tendency to believe that every increase in power means 'an increase of "progress" itself', an advance in 'security, usefulness, welfare and vigour . . . [and] an assimilation of new values into the stream of culture' as if reality, goodness and truth automatically flow from technological and economic power as such."[25] Human beings need to be more aware of and concerned for the ethical implications of technological developments, innovations, and disruptions that people such as Elon Musk embody. "The fact is that 'contemporary man has not been trained to use power well,' because our immense technological development has not been accompanied by a development in human responsibility, values and conscience."[26]

Hope in Catholic social thought would therefore be more circumspect and thoughtful than design thinking's optimism regarding the contributions of new technologies and developments towards progress, guided by *shalom*. Hope in Catholic social thought cautions design thinking's optimism—which may, at times, embody the technocratic paradigm and disruptions that Francis warns against. The iterative process of design thinking acknowledges the less than straightforward nature of finding responses for social issues and therefore holds promise for helping Catholic justice seekers unearth new possibilities and creative solutions. However, practitioners ought to reflect on the proposed solutions and whether they would lead to the genuine well-being of all the various stakeholders, or whether a project only seemingly helps the many, but actually benefits only the few—or none at all.

For example, several companies have been lauded for supposedly disrupting or innovating in their industries, as in the cases of Airbnb and Uber, which drastically changed the hospitality and public transport industries, respectively. These innovations were supposed to benefit both consumers and suppliers in said industries. However, the way both these businesses were set up instead arguably led to more problems, including less accountability, more pollution, and urban sprawl.[27] Facebook, the social media giant, was also initially lauded as innovative and has changed

25. Francis, *Laudato Si'*, sec. 105.
26. Francis, *Laudato Si'*, sec. 105.
27. Matthews, "Sharing Economy Boom Is about to Bust."

the way we connect and communicate with friends and family, replacing earlier iterations such as MySpace and Friendster in popularity. However, Facebook's vast structure has unintentionally contributed to problems related to disinformation that is then manipulated by other businesses, organizations, or politicians for political and economic gain, to the detriment of the ordinary person.[28]

Second, design thinking's optimism is rather more anthropocentric than Christian hope. Optimism in design thinking is convinced of the possibility of change based on the creativity and actions of human beings. As long as human beings cooperate with each other and keep innovating in new and creative ways, positive change can be effected, and a better world is possible.

Hope in Catholic social thought, however, does not place all the stress on human labor. While human action is an important part of the process, hope makes room for grace, which transcends—but can infuse—the realm of human action. Christian hope acknowledges that the end goals of wellbeing and peace are not simply the product of the human action but are also grace—gifts from God that are unmerited and unearned. While humanity bears the responsibility of acting and working towards the common good, Christian hope also brings with it the surrender of faith, where a sense of calm or peace emerges from the recognition that not everything is dependent on human action alone. While many people outside of the Catholic and Christian traditions might disagree, this idea of grace is intrinsic to the hope that orients Catholics in their work towards justice and the ultimate goal and vision of flourishing for all, and it differentiates the stance of Catholic social thought from that of secular design thinkers.

Understanding, Use of Conflict, and Risk

We also need to discuss the conflict and risk in both disciplines, especially since risk and conflict are part of the process of disrupting contemporary systems and structures. These are present when businesses bring in new ideas and business models that challenge the way things are and help people imagine new and conceivably better ways to be and do as a community towards the common good. The importance as well of attending to

---

28. Francis, "Facebook's Ethical Problem."

Design Thinking and Catholic Social Thought

and understanding conflict and risk is heightened in a world that has been constantly described as a VUCA world.[29]

One of the key tenets of design thinking is to provide a loose structure and method to the often-messy process of complex problem-solving and to acknowledge that solutions do not appear immediately nor in a linear way. This is a direct result of the many complexities that human beings experience with their relationships with each other and the world. Design thinking acknowledges that finding solutions to complex societal and ethical issues is not as straightforward as it may seem. There are no predetermined steps that result in a clear solution that immediately works and solves the problem. Aware of the complexities of wicked problems and human limitations, design thinking practitioners acknowledge that the solutions generated may improve situations, but these would not exhaustively solve all the aspects of the problem. It can, perhaps, even cause new issues to spring up that require their own responses—hence the need for continuous iteration.

On the side of Catholic social thought, those seeking to address emerging social problems attempt to find solutions to problems with, as philosopher Gabriel Marcel says, "creative fidelity" to the Catholic tradition.[30] This kind of creativity is not an "anything-goes" type of creativity, as it still remains bound by doctrines and ethical practices in the Catholic tradition. Rather, it consists of a wealth of resources to draw from in dealing with ethical issues including written texts, such as Scripture and magisterial documents, methods, and frameworks, such as casuistry, and other important theological sources and discussions. These are joined by the histories, narratives, and examples of people and communities who have sought to articulate Catholic principles and doctrines and, in response to specific issues, draw from them concrete ways of living and acting that are in line with the Catholic vision of a good life.

Catholic social thought also seeks to provide structure to the messiness of finding solutions to unprecedented problems, as disruptors do in business. However, theologians and practitioners within the Catholic church disagree about the processes and forms of organization through which to do this. As stated earlier, official church leadership and moral teaching, especially on sexual issues, tends to be top-down in its rhetorical and organizational approach, and is often averse to conflicts, difference,

---

29. Recall that VUCA stands for Volatile, Uncertain, Complex, and Ambiguous, which, as an acronym, has been used to describe the current social and environmental milieu.

30. Marcel, *Creative Fidelity*.

and risk.³¹ "Official Catholic social teaching has always seen itself as speaking *for* the whole church.... [T]he Catholic approach claims to teach in a binding manner for the whole church."³²

In the years following the Second Vatican Council, there has been movement from this hierarchical model by emphasizing the *sensus fidei* and the church as a "listening church."³³ Writing in the 1980s, Charles E. Curran argued that in teachings about war and nonviolence, for example, "Catholic social teaching will have to recognize a greater pluralism" and diversity not just in the content of church teaching, but also in the way these teachings are formulated.³⁴ He has also discussed other shifts he saw unfolding since Vatican II such as the "shift to the person, with an emphasis on freedom, equality, and participation" and the shift to relationality and responsibility rather than deontological ethics, all of which have contributed to more development to Catholic social teaching.³⁵

Theologians have also suggested an alternative approach by lifting up experiences of people and communities on the ground that may point to the need to nuance or even reconsider church teaching. This includes how the church hierarchy responds to unique and enculturated contemporary issues because of the doctrinal nature of the religion. There is a tendency to impose a uniform and blanket decision that is firm and clear rather than allowing a more organic and participative process of finding solutions. While the church magisterium's top-down approach to its teaching might be well meaning in its intention to draw from its rich tradition to communicate with clarity and consistency, this approach also implies an uneasiness with messiness and ambiguity. Conservative Catholic groups also expect and prefer clear doctrine and ethics to follow so as not to confuse the faith community.

Catholic theologians have described the tension between an approach focused on clear doctrinal answers and one that navigates the ambiguities and complexities of contemporary moral problems in terms of two different mindsets. Each one yields a distinctive framework for ethical thinking: "classicism" and "historicism." In classicism "one can apprehend man abstractly through a definition that applies *omni et soli* and through

---

31. See Curran, "Catholic Social and Sexual Teaching," 436–37.
32. Curran, "Century of Catholic Social Teaching," 162.
33. Francis, *Pope Calls for a 'Listening Church*.
34. Curran, "Century of Catholic Social Teaching," 159.
35. Curran, "Catholic Social and Sexual Teaching," 429–32.

properties verifiable in every [person]. . . . [I]t follows, in the first place, that on this view one is never going to arrive at any exigence for change."[36] In historicism, on the other hand "one can apprehend mankind as a concrete aggregate developing over time, where the locus of development . . . is the expansion . . . of meaning and of meaningful performance. . . . [and] through this medium . . . that divine revelation has entered the world and that the church's witness is given it."[37]

According to James Keenan, "for classicists, the world is a finished product and truth has already been revealed, expressed, taught, and known. In order to be a truth, it must be universal and unchanging. Clarity is key. Its logic is deductive—we apply the principle to the situation and we derive an answer from the syllogism. . . . [C]hange in moral teaching is, then, problematic; it suggests that at one point a teaching was right and, in a later (or earlier) instance, wrong."[38] Keenan describes how classicists resist contextualization, because it may sound like cultural relativism.[39] "Local diversity and pluralism are seen as threats to the unity and authority of the church."[40] Catholic historicists, on the other hand, acknowledge that, while there is an objective truth, human beings are only gradually "discovering" the truth in history "over time, through experience, and with maturity" because of human limitations.[41] "Moreover, though historicists believe in the importance of the situation and of circumstances, they are not situational ethicists . . . they are modest about their judgements and assertions, and usually quite tentative about any truth-claim; they tend away from clarity . . . and are much more inclined to context."[42]

Both classicist and historicist ways of thinking are present in modern Catholic teaching and Catholic social thought. On the one hand, Scripture and Tradition serve as rich resources for reflecting on the contemporary situation. On the other hand, it can be difficult to choose insights from these resources to bring into dialogue with the current context and what should be learned from the dialogue. Identifying what principles and hermeneutics to prioritize, as well as taking context seriously when reading

36. Lonergan, *Second Collection*, 6.
37. Lonergan, *Second Collection*, 7.
38. Keenan, *Catholic Moral Theology*, 111.
39. Keenan, *Catholic Moral Theology*, 111.
40. Curran, "Catholic Social and Sexual Teaching," 429.
41. Keenan, *Catholic Moral Theology*, 113.
42. Keenan, *Catholic Moral Theology*, 113–14.

and interpreting Scripture and Tradition, are important. Attending to these ongoing tasks is necessary as Christians seek a more holistic and helpful interpretation of religious sources that does not apply the sources in ways that possibly do violence to creation, human or otherwise.[43]

As Catholic thinkers and activists navigate ethical issues, there can be, at times, tension between staying faithful to the many different strands and traditions in Catholic doctrine and creating new and innovative ways of dealing with concrete problems that arise from specific contexts. Because Catholic communities or the Catholic hierarchy see themselves more in the classicist mode, they will tend to shy away from innovation, ambiguity, and complexity, and lessen the possibilities of finding or embracing groundbreaking and positively disruptive kinds of solutions to pressing ethical issues.

CONTRIBUTIONS OF DESIGN THINKING AND CATHOLIC SOCIAL THOUGHT TO BUSINESS ETHICS

Design Thinking's Contribution to Catholic Social Thought

Based on these three spaces for dialogue, design thinking can offer two specific contributions to Catholic social thought in the area of economics and business ethics for more ethical disruption: (1) encouraging interdisciplinarity and collaborative thinking among business people, theologians, and ethicists; and (2) offering a concrete method for Catholic social thought to understand and handle conflict in more productive and life-giving ways.

Encouraging Interdisciplinarity and Collaboration among Business People, Theologians, and Ethicists

First, design thinking can help theologians and ethicists articulate key principles of Catholic social thought in ways that business people can more readily understand. These principles can make it easier for them to hopefully understand and employ Catholic thought in analyzing opportunities for disruption and to do better business. Since scholars and practitioners in both the managerial and social sciences are familiar with design thinking in their respective disciplines, theologians and ethicists can utilize the

---

43. Bordoni, "Pope Francis."

language of design thinking to facilitate effective interdisciplinary work between theology and business. This work, however, goes beyond mere translation. Rather, bringing together these two disciplines is part of the larger interdisciplinary effort needed to articulate the complexity of the present problems in business and to move towards fresh solutions and innovations, with both disciplines contributing to more accurate definitions of the problems involved.

Much contemporary work in business ethics has sought to emphasize the importance of interdisciplinarity. Recent research argues against a prevalent "silo mentality" where business people and scholars in various disciplines simply work in their own fields without engaging with other people outside their specialization areas.[44] These scholars and practitioners advocate for a "lowering of the walls" between disciplines for more exchanges of ideas between fields. People must learn from each other and avoid the insularity that leads to "groupthink." This term refers to situations where participants tend to agree with each other and downplay any disagreements, either because they all come from the same background and context. Thus, they tend to have the same blind spots, or there is a tendency to prioritize harmony and minimize conflict.[45] Interdisciplinarity aims to ameliorate "groupthink" by diversifying the contexts and ideas shared in a given project and encouraging more ideas and considerations to surface. At the same time, advocates of interdisciplinarity know that conflicting ideas will possibly emerge and so promote the use of conflict management tools to constructively handle any disagreements that may arise.

In design thinking, interdisciplinarity is linked with creativity, which entails the capacity to make previously undiscovered connections among different disciplines and concepts. The structural changes needed to move towards a business economy that serves the common good will require cooperative, fruitful, and open relationships among various people, communities, and institutions. Such relationships in the intellectual arena are what interdisciplinarity seeks to foster. Through these relationships, a meaningful exchange of ideas will be created that generates a helpful synthesis. This synthesis can offer new ideas and new ways of thinking through problems and how to address them. These relationships widen the imagination and

---

44. See Gleeson, "Silo Mentality."

45. Currie et al., "Call for University-Based Business Schools to 'Lower Their Walls,'" 742–55.

the alternatives that are practical and possible, rather than limiting the people to already-known successes and failures.

A Concrete Method to Understand and Handle Conflict

Second, design thinking's understanding of and approach to conflict in grappling with complex situations illuminate ways that conflict might fit positively into the vision of integral human development that Catholic social thought offers to business. Disruption and innovation are rife with situations where conflict may arise, where goals and intentions may not be towards the common good, and risks will need to be taken amidst uncertainty. In design thinking, conflict is understood to be part of the process, but it should not be avoided. Rather, it must be managed in ways that are productive and allow for growth. When design thinking practitioners bring together different people from various disciplines with an array of viewpoints and assumptions, disagreements are bound to arise. Design thinking creates a space where practitioners who find themselves disagreeing can clarify the real issues at stake and the differences that need to be resolved, by honestly debating, listening to, and learning from each other.

A top-down method either imposes one solution in a deductive manner, or in an authoritarian manner, where those who disagree are forced to follow without involving them or hearing their concerns and disagreements. Design thinking seeks to cultivate a more inductive and fully participative way of generating solutions. The design thinking process aims to harness "buy-in" and commitment from those who will be implementing or be affected by the solution. Instead of simply shutting down those whose ideas may differ from theirs, participants in the process also learn how to negotiate the different goods at stake and make short-term compromises in order to secure the long-term good of all stakeholders. Places where compromise can be made, and places where there are absolutes that cannot be contravened need to be identified.

From there, negotiations to manage the tension can be undertaken, especially in places where a "stalemate" occurs. Questions can be raised about needs or concerns that must be fulfilled immediately and the ones that can be deferred, given the constraints of limited resources and multiple stakeholders. Questions can also be raised about whether certain stakeholders, their concerns, and their needs, are consistently and disproportionately eclipsed in favor of others. Solutions that come about from this round of discussions will be imperfect because they do not satisfy all the wants or even needs of the stakeholders immediately, given the limitations that are usually present. Because design thinking is an iterative process, this imperfect solution may serve as a starting point for future iterations that could come closer to satisfying the short- and long-term needs of all stakeholders.

From the theological-ethical perspective of this work, conflict can play a role in creating conditions for what I am describing as structures of grace or solidarity. Design thinking can help people manage that conflict in efforts to resist structures of sin and build more gracious and solitary structures. Conflict, as design thinking seeks to demonstrate, is not necessarily sinful nor detrimental to the common good. It can help point to differences in people's assumptions, situations, and ways of understanding problems and make it possible to uncover what truly needs to be addressed. Design thinking also offers a way for participants to raise their concerns and articulate their differences that allows for genuine subsidiarity and that takes their feedback seriously.

Rather than avoid conflict, Catholic social teachers and ethicists can study how conflict might help encourage the generation of new ideas for serving the common good, both on an individual and structural level. Debates on conflicting theological and ethical ideas can help deepen people's faith commitment since they are involved in bringing together theology into conversation about current issues. These conversations can help the community articulate tensions with the tradition and with current socio-economic and political issues and create space for generating the possible solutions or strategies to move towards a structure of grace or solidarity.

CATHOLIC SOCIAL THOUGHT'S CONTRIBUTION TO DESIGN THINKING

Catholic social thought, on the other hand, can offer the following insights to help design thinking practitioners implement the design thinking principles towards ethical disruption: (1) redefine business to guide the design thinking process; and (2) work with design thinkers to ensure genuine participation among the stakeholders involved in business.

A Redefinition of Business That Can Guide the Design Thinking Process

Catholic social thought's understanding of business and the political economy recalibrates the understanding of business that balances the profit motive with feasibility and desirability and disrupts the current extreme focus on profitability and growth. The overall vision of society, as expressed in the Catholic concept of the common good, can help serve as a guide and goal for design thinking, rather than just leaving that goal up to the whims of the participants in any particular design thinking process.[46] When a Catholic social thought perspective is employed, business's purpose is no longer merely limited to maximizing stockholder value. Rather, it becomes more focused on addressing the needs of all those embedded within the business's structures, and how actions of the business might affect those relationships and systems.

Catholic social thought's vision and principles also remind design thinking practitioners of what the common good looks like, and the role of business in such a common good. Guided by this notion of the common good, the design thinking group articulates its vision as inclusive of the well-being of the whole group, to recommend a fair distribution of goods for the stakeholders as an essential part of their goals, and be especially concerned for those stakeholders who are not part of the process or who are at risk of not getting their just shares. Rather than focusing too much on the need of one particular stakeholder or group of stakeholders, Catholic social thought puts into perspective the ways in which the different needs of different stakeholders are intimately interrelated. If the common good is to be served, then addressing the need of one stakeholder entails addressing the needs of others as well.

Such a definition of the common good need not necessarily use explicitly theological language, nor does it require complete consensus. As Christian ethicist Willis Jenkins writes concerning the example of human rights, an articulation "needs to generate just enough shared commitment to cooperate across difference, and should focus on cultivating provisional norms for that cooperation."[47] Rather than focusing on a shared ontology,

---

46. As mentioned earlier, path dependency is a concept that is used to understand whether a particular system can continue despite changes within the community. Catholic social thought can thus offer this vision of the common good as what "path stickiness" can help move a community towards.

47. Jenkins, *Future of Ethics*, 115.

Jenkins notes, the focus is on the continued performance and practice, in this case, of what constitutes the common good. From there, a definition emerges, even if it is always shifting and being reformed, which underpins the ongoing work towards the common good. Through continued practice and drawing from past work, participants can set precedents for the future by further refining what the common good looks like in the face of new contexts and situations.

Ensuring Genuine Participation

Design thinking's treatment of participation can be helpfully oriented by incorporating the concepts of solidarity and subsidiarity that Catholic social thought espouses, as well as attention to both the individual and structural issues at work, in order to ground the disruptive and innovative process. Solidarity, as described in the first chapter, is a firm commitment towards the common good and is not achieved simply through the imposition of doctrine. Working towards the common good, rather, entails practices and structures of subsidiarity, which, as mentioned, takes seriously the concerns and contributions of all stakeholders. Embracing these principles of subsidiarity and solidarity can help keep design thinking on track towards the common good. The incorporation of solidarity and subsidiarity ought to happen not only at the individual level but also at the structural level.

While researchers and practitioners in both design thinking and Catholic social thought have often failed, in practice, to ensure genuine participation, certain streams in Catholicism that advocate for and show concrete ways of practicing subsidiarity are promising. An example would be the Francis's historic appointment of several women to the Vatican congregation that oversees religious orders and his remarks of care and support for the LGBTQ+ community. One can see some openness towards a more inclusive and listening posture and openness to dialogue in navigating ethical and ecclesial issues, particularly under the direction of Francis's papacy.[48] These inroads towards a more socially engaged and participative Catholic church and the different ways some Catholic organizations and communities model subsidiarity in their businesses or non-profits illustrate ways that more inclusive participation can lead businesses towards

---

48. McElwee, "Theologians Praise Pope's Historic Appointment"; O'Loughlin, "While Homosexuality Is Still Illegal."

better solutions to address contextual problems.[49] Business and organizational models inspired by Catholic social thought, such as the Focolare movement's "Economy of Communion," can serve as resources for those who engage in design thinking and to better ensure that all participants are heard and are able to contribute and exchange ideas. These ideas can then be refined to create the best possible responses to problems they have identified.

CONCLUSION: CONCRETELY SYNTHESIZING DESIGN THINKING AND CATHOLIC SOCIAL THOUGHT FOR ETHICAL DISRUPTION

Bringing design thinking and Catholic social thought in conversation in order to help business ethicists and practitioners clarify what structures of sin or injustice are, and how one can resist and ethically disrupt structures of sin in business is the goal. Insights and resources that emerge from the dialogue between design thinking and Catholic social thought can help better describe what might be going wrong in business practice. In particular, it is to help people perceive and analyze unethical patterns that Catholic social thought calls structures of sin. From the design thinking perspective, understanding sinful structures as wicked problems can help tease out the complex relationships and characteristics that make these issues difficult to solve. Teasing out these relationships prepares those attempting to respond to structures of sin to be more cautious as well as be more holistic in how they address these systemic problems and make alternative systems of doing business more mainstream.

The intersection of design thinking and Catholic social thought is also a rich site for ideas to converse and build on each other. This is especially ideal in crafting an ethical methodology for businesses to employ as they review and seek to improve their business practices towards the common good, given their available resources and positions in challenging the dominant narrative in the market. On the one hand, their overlapping ideas provide common ground for the two disciplines to collaborate on a methodology. On the other hand, their points of divergence can be opportunities for the disciplines to further develop through learning from each other, or from other disciplines. To use theological and design thinking

---

49. See Gallagher and Buckeye, *Structures of Grace*; Baxter, "Boosting Resilience and Independence in Kenya."

language, this interchange can help provide ideas and insights for generating strategies that can respond to the wicked problems business face and move businesses from structures of sin towards something better. What this "something better" might look like in the concrete, as well as the best practices that businesses can follow in their efforts to move away from wicked problems and structures of sin, will be discussed in the next chapter.

CHAPTER 5

An Ethic of Disruption Towards Structures of Grace

USING CATHOLIC SOCIAL THOUGHT and design thinking can also uncover fresh resources for rectifying problematic structural conditions. Specifically, this can be done by creating beneficent systems and practices that genuinely disrupt the status quo, which some Catholic social ethicists describe as "structures of grace." In this chapter, a "structure of grace" is defined as a system, institutional practice, or organizational arrangement that: (1) promotes dignity and equitable participation, empowering people by making ethical choices possible and accessible; (2) encourages the development of people's preferences for choosing ethical choices and virtue; and (3) incorporates continuous work to better approximate its beneficent aims, thereby contributing to the ongoing transformation of structures for the common good and the flourishing of creation in the face of complex, unprecedented problems.[1]

As noted earlier, the theological term "grace" in structures of grace implies that creating such structures is not the work of human beings alone, but also involves something unmerited, given by God, which elevates human action.[2] Liberation theologian José Comblin emphasizes the transcendent aspect of structures of grace, and describes grace as "the presence of the future" embodied and lived out through relationships and

---

1. The flourishing of creation intended here refers not only to the development of human beings but also the wider created world.

2. Aquinas, *Summa Theologica* I-II.Q113; Rahner, *Grace in Freedom*; Segundo, *Grace and the Human Condition*; Haight, *Experience and Language of Grace*; Johnson, "Spirit-Sophia," 124–49.

An Ethic of Disruption Towards Structures of Grace

communities—"in the multiplicity of its interwoven activities the diversity of the gifts of the Spirit are manifest."[3] This communitarian, future-oriented aspect of grace "produces resistance, faith, and hope" and is manifested in the "solidarity of actions by human beings."[4]

Another liberation theologian, Margaret Burke, also talks about "activating" one's consciousness of this grace, which is the grace to acknowledge one's complicity in structures of sin and the collective responsibility to take action to resist or transform them. For Burke, understanding this grace requires a deeper sense of "four major aspects of human experience: the personal, interpersonal, societal, and ecological aspects" in order for the person to move from "apathy or helplessness (or both) to hope and determination in the face of a structure [of sin]."[5]

This Christian understanding of grace, as communal, as given, and as interacting with human freedom and action that illumines the fact that work towards creating structures of grace, is both a gift and a task. Seen theologically, this work is something that is always in progress and manifests itself in the particular ways a business organizes its activities. At the same time, its aims will be fully realized only in the eschaton.[6] In different times and places, the work of human beings can either impede or contribute to this fulfillment. One way people are invited to contribute is by creating, preserving, and strengthening structures of grace in their particular contexts. Thus, we will focus on the kind of work we can do in cooperation with said grace.

We will first discuss Catholic social thought on structures of grace, keeping in mind the treatment of structures of sin in the first chapter and drawing from magisterial documents as well as selected theologians. Then, we will draw on the concepts and critiques of Catholic social thought and of design thinking highlighted in previous chapters. Then, we will lay out the principles that businesses might work towards fostering and embodying structures of grace and resisting or dismantling structures of sin. We'll identify three specific principles and practices that such businesses would undertake at various points in the business value chain: first, that the vision, mission, and strategy are tied to stakeholder's well-being with genuine stakeholder participation; second, that there is effective use of conflict and

---

3. Ellacuría and Sobrino, *Mysterium Liberationis*, 525.
4. Ellacuría and Sobrino, *Mysterium Liberationis*, 530.
5. Burke, "Social Sin and Social Grace," 41–42.
6. Dicastery for Promoting Integral Human Development, "Vocation of the Business Leader"; Paul VI, *Populorum Progressio*; Francis, *Laudato Si'*.

risk management using innovation and creativity, grounded in the first principle; and lastly, there is ongoing, value-focused evaluation and iteration, grounded in the first and second principles.

STRUCTURES OF GRACE

The understanding of structures of sin presented previously can be summarized as follows: a structure of sin in a business setting is understood as: "1) a structure that violates human dignity by oppressing human beings and creating a power imbalance between an elite few and the rest of the relevant group or society; 2) a situation that promotes individual selfishness," the formation of vice in persons; or a pattern of 3) habitual and unnoticed "complicity or silent acquiescence when confronted with social injustice," such as the situations of moral complicity in economic life described by Barrera and Finn.[7] Theologians who embrace this understanding of structures of sin have also sought to describe what the opposite of such structures would look like, and thus what Christians might work and hope for. While this chapter is using the traditional term of "grace" to describe these structures opposite to structures of sin, other theologians have proposed or employed different terms in order to more fully capture or to make the kinds of structures towards which Christians are working.

The concept of "structures of grace" does not appear explicitly in modern Catholic social teaching, but it does discuss many important elements of a structure of grace. The magisterial documents offer conditions and descriptions of the kinds of structures that societies should work towards as they seek to overcome structures of sin and the negative effects, such structures have on human communities and on creation. Building on these documents' treatment of structures of sin and of these concepts, theologians have further defined what structures of grace are, and what such structures would look like in practice.

Structures of Grace in Magisterial Documents

Rerum Novarum (1891) and *Quadragesimo Anno* (1931)

Both *Rerum Novarum* and *Quadragesimo Anno* touch on the sinful aspects of the social institutions in their particular times. They both discuss the

---

7. Whitehead and Whitehead, "Attending to the Experience of Injustice," 128–29.

importance of creating and upholding structures that benefit the common good. For Leo XIII, those involved in the state should ensure that the "laws and institutions . . . realize public well-being and private prosperity."[8] Associations that operate for the betterment of workers, for example, should have good governance, and such "rules and organization as may best conduce to the attainment of their respective objects," as they carefully consider the context of the organization.[9]

Pius XI, writing from the context of the great depression in the 1930s and quoting Leo XIII, also argues that social institutions, including but not limited to the state, must be improved upon so that "through the entire scheme of laws and institutions . . . both public and individual well-being may develop spontaneously out of the very structure and administration of the State."[10] Pius XI thus pushes for an institutional structure that includes a sound economy where people are able to earn decent wages and live off their income. At the same time, such an economy should help lead people to God and foster peaceful relations among citizens, in tandem with a state that promotes harmony among diverging classes.[11]

These early documents of modern Catholic social teaching already point to some characteristics of what a structure of grace might look like. Given their particular historical and intellectual contexts, harmony and well-being are stressed as key conditions that institutional structures, such as the state, should create for people.

Mater et Magistra (1961) and *Pacem in Terris* (1963)

In his two social encyclicals, while John XXIII acknowledges that "it is not possible to give a concise definition of the kind of economic structure which is most consonant with man's dignity and best calculated to develop in him a sense of responsibility," he nevertheless identifies characteristics of that might mark such a structure.[12]

First, economic, and other social structures should be organized in ways that safeguard the rights of human beings and foster community. In *Pacem in Terris*, for structures and institutions to truly serve and do good,

8. Leo XIII, *Rerum Novarum*, sec. 32.
9. Leo XIII, *Rerum Novarum*, sec. 56.
10. Pius XI, *Quadragesimo Anno*, sec. 25.
11. Pius XI, *Quadragesimo Anno*, secs. 81–82, 136.
12. John XXIII, *Mater et Magistra*, sec. 84.

they must solve problems that arise with competence, without disregarding the moral law, and with justice and fairness.[13] John XXIII notes that public authorities and institutions, as part of the moral order, should have "a structure and efficacy which make such institutions capable of realizing the common good by ways and means adequate to the changing historical conditions," especially given the complex and evolving problems faced in the modern and global context.[14]

Gaudium et Spes (1965)

In addition to key discussions of human dignity, human rights, and the common good, *Gaudium et Spes* gives special attention to the role of culture. Culture is a vital consideration when it comes to addressing and developing the systems and structures of public institutions and of society. "A change in attitudes and in human structures frequently calls accepted values into question;" and such values are often tied to the kind of culture cultivated in a community, wherein they are often imbibed unconsciously and unquestioned, as well as taught through such things as symbols, art, and language in the community.[15]

Gaudium et Spes describes culture as "the cultivation of the goods and values of nature" where human beings "render social life more human both in the family and the civic community, through improvement of customs and institutions."[16] Through such cultivation, values, assumptions, and ways of living are developed.

The Second Vatican Council also recognized the variety in cultures across the world. This is a fact which, as Kenneth Himes notes, called for greater epistemological humility on the church's part when discussing complex social problems and ethical issues.[17] *Gaudium et Spes* also urges that "human culture must evolve today in such a way that it can both develop the whole human person and aid man in those duties to whose fulfillment all are called."[18] The development of institutions and underlying move-

---

13. John XXIII, *Pacem in Terris*, sec. 69.
14. John XXIII, *Pacem in Terris*, sec. 136.
15. Second Vatican Council, *Gaudium et Spes*, sec. 7; Massingale, *Racial Justice and the Catholic Church*, 32.
16. Second Vatican Council, *Gaudium et Spes*, sec. 53.
17. Himes et al., *Modern Catholic Social Teaching*, loc. 10061–68.
18. Second Vatican Council, *Gaudium et Spes*, sec. 56.

ments is to be a collaboration and product of mutual dialogue between the church and the different disciplines and secular institutions. In engaging and developing culture more fully alongside other public institutions, human beings are cooperating with God:

> When man develops the earth by the work of his hands or with the aid of technology, in order that it might bear fruit and become a dwelling worthy of the whole human family and when he consciously takes part in the life of social groups, he carries out the design of God manifested at the beginning of time, that he should subdue the earth, perfect creation and develop himself. At the same time he obeys the commandment of Christ that he place himself at the service of his brethren.[19]

Culture, which forms the backdrop of assumptions that underlie systems and structures, is to be placed at the service of human beings and the good of society, as well as structures in economic and political life. "The political community can . . . adopt a variety of concrete solutions in its structures and the organization of public authority," but the council stresses that "these solutions must always contribute to the formation of a type of man who will be cultivated, peace-loving and well-disposed towards all his fellow men."[20] Through well-ordered structures and cultures that develop the human being in line with God's work and desires for creation, society can promote and realize peace and justice.[21]

Populorum Progressio (1967)

Paul VI's work on integral human development elaborated further the council's references to developing the human person within the context of society and its various structures. The need for developing countries is not only to receive political freedom, but also to create and "acquire the social and economic structures and processes that accord with man's nature and activity, if their citizens are to achieve personal growth and if their country is to take its rightful place in the international community."[22] This process has often involved clashes between the traditional culture of a community, and the modern technology and institutions that may help development

19. Second Vatican Council, *Gaudium et Spes*, sec. 57.
20. Second Vatican Council, *Gaudium et Spes*, sec. 74.
21. Second Vatican Council, *Gaudium et Spes*, sec. 78.
22. Paul VI, *Populorum Progressio*, sec. 6.

projects in the community. In finding ways to negotiate such conflicts, Paul VI warns against leaving behind traditional culture "without finding any place [for the older moral, spiritual, and religious values] in the new scheme of things."[23]

Populorum Progressio identifies the characteristics of genuine integral human development, which for Paul VI, aside from material well-being, include "broadening the horizons of knowledge . . . a growing awareness of other people's dignity . . . an active interest in the common good, and a desire for peace."[24] "The ultimate goal is a full-bodied humanism" that entails development of the individual and society as a whole, including systemization and industrial organization.[25] For Paul VI, society requires structures that are in accord with human nature and activity. Such structures would encourage integral human development that is holistic and not reductionary of human nature.

Laborem Exercens (1981) and *Centesimus Annus* (1991)

John Paul II touches on the importance of beneficent structures in *Laborem Exercens* when he discusses proposals on how economic and businesses might be restructured to ensure work conditions that are not oppressive and help develop individuals. Some examples of this include "proposals for joint ownership of the means of work, sharing by the workers in the management and/or profits of business, [and] so-called shareholding by labor."[26]

In *Centesimus Annus*, John Paul II, reflecting upon the fall of communism, elaborates on the context of the emerging social structures in the latter part of the twentieth century, describing the important, productive, but "difficult . . . transition towards more participatory and more just political structures."[27] *Centesimus Annus* reiterates the importance of structures that are just, underscores human rights, and encourages participation from below and shared responsibility in order to work towards integral human development. There is an importance of developing positive structures within nations, "so that each nation can uphold its own rights and reach a

23. Paul VI, *Populorum Progressio*, sec. 10.
24. Paul VI, *Populorum Progressio*, sec. 21.
25. Paul VI, *Populorum Progressio*, secs. 26, 42–43.
26. John Paul II, *Laborem Exercens*, sec. 14.
27. John Paul II, *Centesimus Annus*, sec. 22.

just agreement and peaceful settlement vis-à-vis the rights of others. . . . A patient material and moral reconstruction is needed, even as people, exhausted by longstanding privation, are asking their governments for tangible and immediate results in the form of material benefits and an adequate fulfillment of their legitimate aspirations."[28] John Paul II also recalls the previous popes' stress on the need for concrete structures, not just at the level of local communities or nations but at the level of international communities. This is due to the effects of globalization on the ways economics, business, and politics are done and the ways relationships are forged among countries.

His previous work on structures of sin exhorts society "to destroy such structures [of sin] and replace them with more authentic forms of living in community . . . which demands courage and patience."[29] Key to this, he affirms, is the family, the first structure, wherein a person grows in relationship with others. It is in this first structure that people begin to develop themselves by learning virtues and their own potential. In addition to the family, the adequate formation of culture is also important; John Paul II states that "the Church promotes those aspects of human behavior which favor a true culture of peace" which can help individuals flourish.[30] Peace is another name for development, speaking of a "collective responsibility for promoting development," and not just avoiding war or evil actions. This culture of peace requires ongoing efforts to increase "mutual understanding and knowledge, and to increase the sensitivity of the conscience."[31] Such a culture of peace and development, also described by John XXIII, forms part of the underlying culture of a structure of grace.

Anticipating the objection that common good-oriented structures would hamper business and technological advancement, *Centesimus Annus* assures that more people-serving and just structures would not "impede but rather promote the greater productivity and efficiency of work itself," even though "it may weaken consolidated power structures."[32]

At the same time, John Paul II acknowledges that the changes he calls for are, in many ways, not compatible with the currently dominant economic system. To offer one important example, John Paul II's development

---

28. John Paul II, *Centesimus Annus*, sec. 27.
29. John Paul II, *Centesimus Annus*, sec. 38.
30. John Paul II, *Centesimus Annus*, sec. 51.
31. John Paul II, *Centesimus Annus*, sec. 52.
32. John Paul II, *Centesimus Annus*, sec. 43.

of the universal destination of goods that circumscribes the right to private property would require a redistribution of power and resources. While some might balk at this, and say that John Paul II is asking people to give up all private property in a purely communist system, he makes it clear that universal destination of goods is not to abolish private property, but rather to ensure that the poor do not go without while others have more than they can spend in a lifetime. To make this possible, those who currently hold power and resources will have to give up at least some of what they own. This can prove difficult because those with power and accustomed to a particular standard of living rarely are willing to give up the power and resources that benefit them.

Like his predecessors, John Paul II highlights the importance of structures that are just, that emphasize collective and shared responsibility, that encourage participation, and that help people develop authentically. Structures that reorient culture as well as the market and the economy towards the common good, and shift that established distribution of power from one wherein power is concentrated among the few, to one that is more participative and that helps build the common good are also important. For John Paul II, structures of grace would safeguard human rights and the development of the common good but may also threaten existing power structures that stand in the way of the common good and that privilege selfishness.

Caritas in Veritate (2009)

In his only social encyclical, Benedict XVI asserts that structures cannot guarantee integral human development without the responsibility and work of people. However, structures are important as instruments in helping or hindering the progress towards personal and social development.[33]

Rather than fatalistically regarding human beings as wholly determined by social forces, the current structures are products of human action and cultures that can also be remolded through concrete action and discernment, continuing John Paul II's theme of focusing on people's actions over systems and structures discussed previously.[34] Social structures ought to be governed by justice and ethics. More specifically, economic structures should reflect "a model of market economy capable of including within

33. Benedict XVI, *Caritas in Veritate*, sec. 17.
34. Benedict XVI, *Caritas in Veritate*, sec. 42.

its range all peoples and not just the better off," and be organized in ways that "without rejecting profit, aim at a higher goal than the mere logic of the exchange of equivalents, of profit as an end in itself."[35] Furthermore, "the proper functioning of any market requires mutual trust and internal solidarity . . . some necessary elements of this are transparency and justice, including the three main types of justice: commutative, distributive, and social justice."[36]

Benedict XVI also emphasizes shared decision-making and power sharing as necessary features of a "political, juridical and economic order . . . for the development of all peoples in solidarity."[37] In order for society to create such structures, he stresses, human beings need to ground themselves in God and not just in themselves. Only a "humanism open to the Absolute" can animate and advance the work for social justice and integral human development, as well as guide the work of building cultures and structures for the common good.[38] Rather than a separation of faith and the sciences, this work entails theologians to engage in solidarity with experts in different disciplines, and more broadly, "challeng[ing] all persons and the global community as a whole to imagine a different path—an economy in which ethics and gift play significant roles."[39]

Notably for this project, Benedict XVI does not limit his analysis to macroeconomic structures, but also explicitly discusses the role businesses play in society. In business management, there is the importance of social responsibility, as well as systems and structures that treat all people with dignity and concern, and not just those who hold power within the organization. Profit should be treated not as an end in itself, but as a means towards the end of a "more humane market and society," and that businesses require "a suitable juridical and fiscal structure" to do so.[40]

In light of the economic crisis that struck in 2008, while he was preparing the encyclical for its delayed release, Benedict specifically uses the area of finance as an example. He urges that financial structures should be renovated in ways that will make finance "an instrument directed towards improved wealth creation and development" for all, rather than subject

---

35. Benedict XVI, *Caritas in Veritate*, secs. 38–39.
36. Clark, "Caritas in Veritate," loc. 16859.
37. Benedict XVI, *Caritas in Veritate*, sec. 67.
38. Benedict XVI, *Caritas in Veritate*, sec. 78.
39. Clark, "Caritas in Veritate," loc. 16743, 16778.
40. Benedict XVI, *Caritas in Veritate*, sec. 46.

to the abuses of excessive speculation.⁴¹ Some examples of good financial structures, such as microfinance institutions and projects, highlight the importance of proper risk management as well as the mutual responsibility of the business and the consumer. Even though Benedict XVI calls for structural reform without direct reference to structural sin, perhaps due to his focus on individual responsibility, he explicitly connects structures of grace with business, and enumerates characteristics that would mark a business as a structure of grace, especially in the realm of finance.⁴²

Evangelii Gaudium (2013), *Laudato Si'* (2015), and *Laudato Deum* (2023)

As Francis discusses in great detail the violence and injustice of sinful social structures today, he also discusses what characterizes good structures. In the apostolic exhortation *Evangelii Gaudium*, Francis emphasizes the priority placed by his papacy on justice and care for the poor while he reiterates and expands on Benedict XVI's emphasis on the importance of a life animated by God for sustaining structures that facilitate development and evangelization.⁴³ Not only does this point to Francis's attentiveness to structures, this also indicates the priority Francis places on the need for a posture of openness towards change for the common good. This openness implies not just change at the level of individual action, but also at the level of systems and structures. He rejects an attitude of complacency that says, "we have always done things a certain way" and "invite[s] everyone to be bold and creative in the task of rethinking goals, structures, styles, and methods" for advancing evangelization and integral human development.⁴⁴

Francis also acknowledges the integral role of women in creating just structures in both the church and in non-religious social arenas, including the workplace.⁴⁵ For him, "changing structures without generating new convictions and attitudes will only ensure that those same structures will become, sooner or later, corrupt, oppressive and ineffectual."⁴⁶ That is why

---

41. Benedict XVI, *Caritas in Veritate*, sec. 65.
42. Clark, "Caritas in Veritate," loc. 16905.
43. Francis, *Evangelii Gaudium*, secs. 26–27.
44. Francis, *Evangelii Gaudium*, sec. 33.
45. Francis, *Evangelii Gaudium*, sec. 103. See Case, "Role of the Popes in the Invention of Complementarity," 155–72; Garbagnoli, "Against the Heresy of Immanence," 187–204.
46. Francis, *Evangelii Gaudium*, sec. 189.

there is a great need to reshape social structures to serve the common good also requires of people a spiritual conversion, along with a change of attitude that entails moral conversion.

In the concluding chapter of *Laudato Si'*, Francis offers several proposals to address structures of sin and work towards structures of grace that can embody the integral ecology he advocates. Moving in this direction, he emphasizes the importance of dialogue and cooperation at the local, national, and international levels. There are United Nations initiatives to address the climate crisis, and these projects are carried out on the ground, as examples of organizations moving towards structures of well-being and grace. These initiatives also directly mitigate the environmental crisis to entail restructuring not just the economic modes of production but also the political systems that govern said modes. For example, the regulation and operation of food production has a direct impact on the condition of the land and air through such things as the fertilizers and chemicals introduced to grow crops. "Agriculture in poorer regions can be improved through investment in rural infrastructures, a better organization of local or national markets, systems of irrigation, and the development of techniques of sustainable agriculture. New forms of cooperation and community organization can be encouraged in order to defend the interests of small producers and preserve local ecosystems from destruction."[47] These changes would help create conditions that more closely resemble a structure of grace rather than sin, where the community of creation—both human and non-human—may flourish.

The capacity to enforce such initiatives, however, is still lacking. There is also a need for solutions to the climate crisis to address both reducing pollution and development of poorer communities.[48] These issues are complex, and a complexity of solutions are also required to tackle those issues.

Similar to design thinking, Francis encourages a multidisciplinary and multi-stakeholder approach to tackling the wicked problems posed by "the cry of the earth and the cry of the poor." He suggests a dialogue between and among politicians, economists, religions, and scientists as an essential element in the pursuit of social and environmental justice. These consonances with design thinking emerge explicitly in Francis's acknowledgement of the connections among different social and ecological issues in *Laudato Si'*, as well as in the synod documents treated in the next section.

47. Francis, *Laudato Si'*, sec. 180.
48. Francis, *Laudato Si'*, sec. 175.

Francis also discusses the importance of creating a new "'model of global development;' this will entail a responsible reflection on the 'meaning of economy and its goals with an eye to correcting its malfunctions and misapplications.'"[49] For Francis, "it is not enough to balance, in the medium term, the protection of nature with financial gain, or the preservation of the environment with progress."[50] It is "redefining our notion of progress. A technological and economic development which does not leave in its wake a better world and an integrally higher quality of life cannot be considered progress."[51] Francis also highlights the importance of the commitment and communion of all stakeholders as part of the kinds of structures that need to be created, and not just to rely on technological remedies and solutions, as seen in his discussion of COP28 and the climate crisis in *Laudato Deum*.[52]

Lastly, and like his immediate predecessors, Francis also points to the importance of changing cultures: the assumptions, attitudes, and anthropologies that underlie the way people think and act. Education and spirituality are important, according to Francis, in order to help people go "out of ourselves and towards the other," to empathize, and to understand the deep interconnection that binds all creation.[53] Thus, it is important attend to culture in thinking about and seeking to foster structures of grace, as well as questioning the assumptions and underlying ideologies behind structures, such as the notion of progress and growth. By turning his attention to the environment explicitly and its connections to other socioeconomic and political issues, he also further fleshes out the issue of the environment and its relationship to structures of sin as well as structures of grace.

Final Document of the Amazon Synod (2019), *Querida Amazonia* (2020), and *Fratelli Tutti* (2020)

The Final Document of the Amazon Synod reiterates the importance of integral conversion. This is defined as a conversion to care for the interrelated issues of the environment and the poor based on synodality, the process of communal discernment and collaboration among the Catholic church hierarchy, in crafting social "structures in harmony with creation"

---

49. Francis, *Laudato Si'*, sec. 194.
50. Francis, *Laudato Si'*, sec. 194.
51. Francis, *Laudato Si'*, sec. 194.
52. Francis, *Laudate Deum*, secs. 57–60.
53. Francis, *Laudato Si'*, sec. 208.

An Ethic of Disruption Towards Structures of Grace

and that truly serve people.[54] "Intercultural, interreligious, and ecumenical dialogue" between church leaders and relevant communities are key elements for creating such structures, and this dialogue especially needs to include the marginalized, and indigenous people.[55] The 2019 synod document recalls the proposals made by Francis in *Laudato Si'* and examines the importance of synodality in crafting those structures:

> In order to walk together, the Church today needs a conversion to the synodal experience. It needs to strengthen a culture of dialogue, reciprocal listening, spiritual discernment, consensus, and communion in order to find areas and ways of joint decision-making and to respond to pastoral challenges. In this way, co-responsibility in the life of the Church will be fostered in a spirit of service. . . . Synodality is a constitutive dimension of the Church. We cannot be Church without recognizing a real practice of the *sensus fidei* of all the People of God.[56]

While Francis discusses synodality in the context of the Catholic church, the culture of dialogue, listening, discernment, and finding common ground can also be applied to structures in business, especially when conflict arises. These are not necessarily just for the Catholic church, but also can be developed in other structures, though it may not necessarily be called synodality outside of the institution of the Catholic church.

Decision-making, from this synodal viewpoint, is a communal task that entails reflection and discernment. The elements mentioned in the quote above are important conditions for moving towards organizational structures that support a more communitarian style of living, one that, for believers, includes reflection on how best to cooperate with God's salvific work in the world.[57] This synodal style of living, the bishops write, should be decentralized at different local and national levels, yet still connected with other church communities. It is "establish[ing] harmony between communion and participation, between co-responsibility and the ministries of all, paying special attention to the effective participation of the laity

---

54. Synod of Bishops for the Pan-Amazon, *Final Document of the Amazon Synod*, sec. 18.

55. Synod of Bishops for the Pan-Amazon, *Final Document of the Amazon Synod*, sec. 48.

56. Synod of Bishops for the Pan-Amazon, *Final Document of the Amazon Synod*, sec. 88.

57. Synod of Bishops for the Pan-Amazon, *Final Document of the Amazon Synod*, secs. 91–92.

in discernment and decision-making, and favoring the participation of women."[58]

Francis also elaborates on the importance of inculturation in creating structures that are life-giving in his 2020 post-synodal exhortation *Querida Amazonia*. Inculturation, like synodality, entails listening to and learning from others, including indigenous peoples. It also includes synthesizing the knowledge and culture of the people with gospel values, in order to create communities that help people to flourish and integrate peacefully and justly with each other, and to resist falling prey to consumerism and isolation.[59]

In *Fratelli Tutti*, Francis states the need for society to be structured "in such a way that everyone has a chance to contribute his or her own talents and efforts."[60] "We must put human dignity back at the centre and on that pillar build the alternative social structures we need" and that such structures can be renewed through a love exercised through the social and political.[61]

Structures of Grace in Select Catholic Theologians' Work

As mentioned earlier, several contemporary theologians have developed further the social aspects of grace. José Comblin, for instance, discusses grace's social characteristics. Leonardo Boff, when thinking about what the institutional church's organization should look like, proposes charisms as the organizing principle of the structure of the Catholic church. He defines charisms as God's gifts to individual human beings that animate the presence of the Holy Spirit in individuals' lives, activities, talents, and among the community. Charisms are a "concrete way in which the Spirit and the risen Lord are present in the world."[62]

Ignacio Ellacuría describes structures of grace as "social historical structures [that] objectify grace and serve as vehicles for that power in favor of human life" as opposed to sinful structures, "social and historical structures that objectify the power of sin and serve as vehicles for that

---

58. Synod of Bishops for the Pan-Amazon, *Final Document of the Amazon Synod*, sec. 92.

59. Francis, *Querida Amazonia*, secs. 70–72.

60. Francis, *Fratelli Tutti*, sec. 162.

61. Francis, *Fratelli Tutti*, sec. 168, 183–86.

62. Boff, *Church*, 156, 159.

An Ethic of Disruption Towards Structures of Grace

power against humanity."[63] Such grace, operating in society, offers a way for "God's potency to achieve a more humane and open history by means of structures, institutions, and social bodies that open human beings more and more to themselves and to others."[64]

Daniel Castillo shares the structures' relationship to grace and liberation and argues for Francis's concept of integral ecology that "calls for the radical transformation of the contemporary globalization project in accordance with God's will."[65] Castillo maps onto integral ecology the concept of integral liberation argued for by Gustavo Gutiérrez, which emphasizes liberation in terms of societal structures, cultures and perspectives, and ultimately salvation from sin. He highlights Francis's thought that there is a "right ordering of the world's political ecology so that it might best serve the common good" and that "the patchwork of superficial responses that Francis identifies cannot attend adequately to the eco-social emergency."[66] Socioeconomic, cultural and psycho-social transformation all need to happen in order for integral ecology to be realized.[67]

Bernard Lonergan offers another useful take on the structural dimensions of the human good and its absence, by way of his descriptions of *scotosis* and cycles of decline. *Scotosis* refers to a systemic blindness that arises from people's biases. Such bias and *scotosis* can lead to historical cycles of decline, which describe how structures of sin take shape in communities as discussed in an earlier chapter. With respect to structures of grace, Lonergan speaks of the factors that contribute to cycles of progress, and to the healing of *scotosis*, in his explanation of *cosmopolis*. He describes the *cosmopolis* as an answer to the cycles of decline and *scotosis* or intellectual blindness. For Lonergan, the *cosmopolis* is a way of organizing community that helps achieve human good and social progress by "prevent[ing] dominant groups from deluding mankind by the rationalization of their sins." He explains that "it is this universalization of the sin by rationalization that contributes to the longer cycle of decline . . . [and which] cosmopolis has to ridicule, explode, destroy."[68]

---

63. Ellacuría, *Historicity of Christian Salvation*, 150.
64. Ellacuría, *Historicity of Christian Salvation*, 153.
65. Castillo, *Ecological Theology of Liberation*, 93–94.
66. Castillo, *Ecological Theology of Liberation*, 107, 114.
67. Castillo, *Ecological Theology of Liberation*, 115.
68. Lonergan, *Insight*, 264.

Acknowledging that the human good is both individual and social, Lonergan describes social progress as the continual flow of improvement "from subjects being their true selves [when] observing the transcendental precepts [of being] attentive, intelligent, reasonable, and responsible."[69] When people are attentive, intelligent, reasonable, and responsible, they are able to create change in the cycles of decline, and "change begets further change and the sustained observance of the transcendental precepts makes these cumulative changes an instance of progress."[70] In order to move away from *scotosis* and cycles of decline and move towards social progress, a community that is structured as *cosmopolis* encourages truth telling in the face of the shifting of power from generation to generation. This is not only just to ensure the halting of cycles of decline, but also to purge false rationalizing and myth making from the cosmopolis itself and its analysts.[71]

As a "dimension of one's consciousness, a heightened grasp of historical origins, a discovery of historical responsibilities," the perspective and practice of cosmopolis is not easy to develop. Its perspective is challenging to foster given that "every *scotosis* [general bias being one example] puts forth a plausible, ingenious, adaptive, untiring resistance" which can make it difficult to even identify what the *scotosis* is and how to address it.[72] Creating the corresponding practices and community of cosmopolis also entails daunting challenges. However, though complicated, it is not impossible. At its deepest levels, the "cosmopolis now becomes not simply a collaboration of men and women with one another, but their cooperation with God in working out the solution to the problem of evil that affects us. This collaboration is primarily God's work."[73]

In the realm of business, Lonergan's contributions shed light on how structures in business might be molded to become more in line with structures of grace. For example, moving to new visions and frameworks of doing business that encourage more transparency and more equal care among stakeholders, and which encourage people in that organization to be more conscientious, responsible, and reasonable, can lead towards sustained change over time. This change can become easier to accomplish once the community is "stuck" to the path, as explained in the concept of

69. Lonergan, *Method in Theology*, 52–53.
70. Lonergan, *Method in Theology*, 53.
71. Lonergan, *Insight*, 265.
72. Lonergan, *Insight*, 266–67.
73. Doran, *Theology and the Dialectics of History*, 203.

path dependency and Lonergan's concept of cycles of progress. There are also promising connections to design thinking, for example, in their shared emphasis on interdisciplinarity and on the inclusion of various viewpoints to help avoid the biases that Lonergan describes. It can be difficult to identify the *scotosis* or blindness at work. When design thinking welcomes different perspectives, collaboration across differences, and proper conflict management, it also fosters an encounter among different people that helps shed light on what possible biases are at work. The description of progress in *cosmopolis* also parallels the iterative process in design thinking, in how change begets change, and can lead the organization in a particular direction.

Using various Christian social movements as examples, theological ethicist Kevin Ahern shows concrete ways such movements are able to counteract structures of sin and thus serve as models of what structures of grace might look like in the world today. Ahern's book describes three Christian social movements—Young Christian Workers, the Jesuit Refugee Service, and the Plowshares—and explains how each one serves the Catholic church's justice mission. Businesses are not non-government organizations in the same way of the movements studied by Ahern's books; there are differences not just legally, but also structurally and financially, and in their organizational missions. However, some questions that Ahern identified for these Christian social movements also apply to businesses, including whether or not a business organization should enter into some form of justice or advocacy work, and how to do that. Would it, for instance, be best to do so by transforming its organization and value chain, by engaging in corporate social responsibility projects, or would it need to do something else?[74]

Ahern takes his cue from John Paul II's description of structures of sin in *Reconciliatio et Paenitentia*. They discuss social sin by detailing that (1) all personal sin can be understood as social sin since there can be no purely personal, private sin that is disconnected from others due to human beings' social nature; (2) social sin also includes sins that are more clearly social and that affect others more directly; and (3) social sin includes those sins present in the relationships between communities and nation-states. The activities of Christian social movements push back against these three forms of social sin and describe the Christian social movements as structures of grace insofar as they are able to: (1) "help individuals open up to

---

74. Ahern, *Structures of Grace*, 58.

the social demands of the gospel"; (2) advocate for "analysis aimed at holding political leaders and institutions accountable to the demands of the common good"; and (3) "seek to transform social, political, and economic relationships to be more in line with the demands of the gospel."[75]

Similar to Ahern's work, John Gallagher and Jeanne Buckeye illustrate ways of identifying structures of grace in business. They recount how certain business's decisions and policies have served the common good and helped their communities grow and develop. They examine businesses that are part of the Economy of Communion movement to identify ways in which businesses can be structures of grace. Their work investigates businesses dedicated to the principles of the Economy of Communion in several different industries, such as Mundell and Associates in environmental care, Eos Finish Line Inc. and La Parola in education, Consort International and Terra Nuova in manufacturing and restoration, and Spiritours in travel and tours. Gallagher and Buckeye describe the different values and principles that guide Economy of Communion businesses when they create their policies in marketing and advertising, finance, human resources, and strategic planning. They emphasize that there is no one-size-fits-all business template that all these Economy of Communion businesses are following. However, they do illustrate some practices these businesses had in common.

While some of these shared practices stemmed from the businesses' adherence to the principles laid out by the Economy of Communion, some also came from the owners' own experiences and understanding of their respective industries. This is a critical point to raise as it helps respond to the criticism that the Economy of Communion may be unrealistic or untenable in the "real world," where the dominant economic system does not necessarily espouse the same ideals. While business owners in the Economy of Communion strive towards the ideals that their spirituality advocates, they also work to make it doable not just by a few, but by all, through dialogue with different disciplines and using existing tools and methods available. The owner of Mundell and Associates, for instance, brings the principles of the Economy of Communion into conversation with his expertise in engineering and the environment. This combination influences the solutions he offers to his clients, which have led to safer communities for people as well as more sustainable ways of being in community that also care for the environment.

---

75. Ahern, *Structures of Grace*, 133–36.

An Ethic of Disruption Towards Structures of Grace

Ethicist Daniel Daly suggests using the terms virtue and vice to highlight the formative nature of social structures on those who participate in them. It is important to emphasize the virtue in the Catholic moral tradition. He uses the term structures of virtue to "situate[e] the concept [of structures] in the framework of virtue, with its rich tradition, and its ability to describe and prescribe moral excellence" as well as "affirm that virtuous social structures inculcate and facilitate the person's acquisition of the virtues."[76] Thus, he defines virtuous structures as "structures that "contain social relations that enable and facilitate a person's performance of virtuous actions and subsequent acquisition and cultivation of the virtues. . . . [Virtuous structures] are those webs of relations that consistently promote the normative human dignity and well-being of all affected by those relations, especially the vulnerable."[77]

Daly's emphasis on the formative aspect of structures dovetails with Ahern's descriptions of the ways Christian social movements engage in ethical formation and consciousness building among their members. Ahern gives examples such as the Young Christian Workers, which "highlights the potential of movements to shape the personal and ethical formation of leaders through cell groups, study sessions, publications, and campaigns," the Jesuit Refugee Services' focus on education that "aim at empowering refuges to be agents of justice and reconciliation," and the Plowshares' witness that seeks to be an invitation "to conversion and to educate . . . about the evils of the weapons industry."[78] Daly's work also resonates with certain businesses in the Economy of Communion. While not all the businesses studied by Gallagher and Buckeye explicitly mention Economy of Communion spirituality in describing the vision and mission of their business, many of the businesses do still engage in ethical formation and discussion. Either they are meeting with and engaging fellow Economy of Communion businesses, or, in some cases, they engage their clients and partners by explaining to them why they do business according to the principles set out by the Focolare spirituality.

---

76. Daly, "Structures of Virtue and Vice," 357.
77. Daly, *Structures of Virtue and Vice*, 168–69.
78. Ahern, *Structures of Grace*, 133–34.

Summary: Structures of Grace in Catholic Social Thought

Especially since the 1980s, Catholic social teaching has developed a vocabulary of structural sin to ethically critique current social systems and institutional structures. While these documents have not explicitly defined structures of grace, they do point to characteristics that mark such structures. Extrapolating these characteristics can enable us to define structures of grace and identify broad principles for pursuing them that can be contextualized, depending on the needs and concerns of the community. This is done with the end goal of helping move communities and organizations towards more closely approximating these beneficent and virtuous structures.

The concepts of structures of sin, and in particular, structures of grace in Catholic social thought continue to be developed by various theologians. While the operation of power in relation to structures of grace has not been explicitly discussed in magisterial documents or fully developed by theologians, the structures of grace being conceived here are structures that are justly empowering for all participants. In these structures, unjust power imbalances present in structures of sin are corrected and guarded. In general, structures of grace correct imbalances in power not through mere domination, or by relying on the power of individuals, but rather by "making God's power present in [history]."[79]

Drawing on Lonergan's concept of cosmopolis, structures of grace should not operate to hide from participants the myth-making and historical revisionism that allow shifts in power from one structure to another. Instead, they should enable people to recognize and interrogate these processes, asking whether and where they are moving towards progress, or decline. Structures of grace work to reveal the truth by encouraging people to think about the implied values and assumptions that underly socioeconomic, political, or business choices, the community they are becoming in validating such choices, and whether or not such choices are actually aligned with the common good. If a business chooses to shift its business model to a model to better serve its stakeholders and the wider community, its strategic choices need to be examined whether they are genuinely benefitting everyone. If, for example, a business that cares for the environment and for stakeholders creates a plan to build a new mall by bulldozing a forest, organizations, mechanisms, or processes that align with structures

---

79. Ellacuría, *Historicity of Christian Salvation*, 156–58.

of grace would pressure or require business leaders to question whether such a move is aligned with its stated stakeholder and environmentally-friendly vision, mission, and strategy. Both internal and external processes, protocols, or organizations to the business that work as its structures of grace would operate to raise red flags and press for accountability. This is crucial, especially if the business attempts to spin its decision on the mall as totally environmentally friendly and as benefitting everyone involved, when the reality is different, or at least is far more complex and ambiguous in the long term.

Based on the above discussion of grace, I would identify structures of grace, especially in the realm of business, by the following characteristics:

Structures of Sin	Structures of Grace
(1) A structure that violates human dignity by oppressing human beings and creating a power imbalance between an elite few and the rest of the relevant group or society	(1) A structure that promotes dignity and equitable participation, empowering people by making ethical choices possible and accessible
(2) A situation that promotes individual selfishness or the formation of vice in persons	(2) A structure that encourages the development of people's preferences for choosing ethical choices and virtue
(3) A pattern of habitual and unnoticed complicity in, or silent acquiescence when confronted with social injustice	(3) A structure that continuously works to better approximate its beneficent aims, thereby contributing to the ongoing transformation of structures for the common good and the flourishing of creation in the face of complex, unprecedented problems

Table 1. Features of Structures of Sin and Structures of Grace

(1) A Structure That Promotes Dignity and Equitable Participation, Empowering People by Making Ethical Choices Possible and Accessible.

This first defining characteristic of structures of grace ensures that all participants have what is needed—including freedom, information, resources, and agency—to exercise actual ethical choice. Some might claim that, when in the business setting, people exercise power mainly as individual consumers by choosing which businesses to patronize. However, the current global economic situation of vast income and wealth inequality skews power heavily towards large or multinational businesses, which are typically controlled by a few, but have the resources and economic scale and synergy to put any project into action.[80] Even though such businesses might offer ethically sourced products, if these same businesses do not make them affordable and accessible, or do not offer fair wages to their employees so they can patronize the more ethical choice, then that ethical choice becomes something only the rich can enjoy. The "unethical" choice becomes the only "real" choice that the middle or poorer classes can access. In relation to the first element of our definition, this type of power imbalance makes it systemically difficult for less-advantaged majorities to practice choosing to do the good.

Many less affluent consumers have to prioritize price over other criteria, frequently leading to a forced choice of patronizing products or services that may not be either just or sustainable. Given their greater power, businesses—especially large and multinational corporations—bear more responsibility to create structures in the market that allow consumers a better and genuine exercise of ethical choice, for example, through creative strategies and innovation of their products and services. As larger organizations, they have more resources, both tangible and non-tangible (e.g., information), that they can marshal for projects compared to what is available to the average consumer. Thus, a structure of grace would help disrupt such a skewed power dynamic in favor of more equitable choices and access to needs and resources, even in increments or through small communities that put these principles into practice.

(2) A Structure That Encourages the Development Virtue and Preferences of Individuals for Making Ethical Choices.

As mentioned by both Daly and Ahern, a structure of grace is formative because it helps people develop virtues rather than vices, to develop a habit a preference for and choice to do the good. For businesses, it means thinking about what virtues and vices their products and organization systems are encouraging. For example, when businesses produce and sell clothes, the business's protocols, processes, or organizations that operate as structures of grace will encourage the decision-makers in the business to think about

---

80. See Peterson, "10 Companies That Control Almost Everything We Eat"; Badenhausen, "World's Most Valuable Brands 2018."

the ways in which their production and marketing activities are promoting a particular lifestyle—and not just superficial fashion lifestyles like being "preppy," "grunge," or "simple." More fundamentally, is the business promoting a "fast fashion" lifestyle where clothes focus more on trends and quick turnaround of cheap clothes that often end up in the landfill after only a few times of usage, or is it promoting "slow fashion," where their clothes are made sustainably and prepared to last a long time? Social media businesses might think not just about how they might improve the technology for networking among people, but also the quality of that networking, versus what is seen currently in the rise of disinformation and political architecture that takes advantage of social media and contributes to socio-economic and political polarization.[81]

Many people already prefer to do the good, for example, by purchasing products that are ethically made and services that are justly remunerated, as seen in the studies cited in the introduction of this book. However, preferring something does not automatically lead to doing. That's why a structure of grace should not just habituate preferences and choice, but also be a space where those choices are available and accessible. That's where the importance of connecting the first element of the definition of structures of grace, with this second element, to disrupt the current ways of doing business that don't necessarily give those choices or that perpetuate particular lifestyle choices that do not habituate or put the common good into practice.

(3) A Structure Where There Is Continuous Work to Better Approximate Its Beneficent Aims for the Transformation of Structures for the Well-Being of Creation in the Face of Complex, Unprecedented Problems.

This last part of the definition encourages continuous work towards the common good and inclusive well-being. Similar to Lonergan's understanding of social progress as continual and to design thinking's iterative process, structures of grace are works in progress. New contexts will entail new issues and cause new questions to arise, concerning the good of the individual and the good of society. A structure of grace is thus always evolving and is never stagnant while a structure of grace that endures over time may become part of a living tradition and not stuck in traditionalism.

81. See Ong and Cabanes, "Architects of Networked Disinformation."

The Ethics of Disruption in Business

A structure of grace thus also encourages people to adapt to and respond to the unprecedented and complex problems that structures of sin pose with creative fidelity to the gospel. Rather than simply create any possible solutions in the name of progress first, and thinking about the ethical implications only afterwards, a structure of grace encourages people to think together about workable solutions and their implications simultaneously, while analyzing the impact that a given solution might genuinely have on all affected. For business people, such analysis would consider the complexity and ethical dimensions of the issue, and not just the physical or financial aspects. Businesses undertaking this kind of analysis would also critically question the business assumptions and systems already at play, asking whether or not these should also be changed.

A structure where transformation continues to happen is also empowering. It can help the participants' charisms—their gifts and talents—flourish and further develop, as both Ahern and Boff mention. For Boff, Spirit-bestowed charisms play a significant role in the Catholic church's structures. Charisms become the organizing principle for ecclesial structures, which helps build community and unites people by integrating the diverse contributions of people. Ahern notes that certain movements and organizations "may also be considered structures of grace in the ways which they embody or seek to institutionalize specific charisms or special graces."[82] Such organizations "continue to be guided their charisms as they continually seek to be placed in the service of the common good," which is built up by not just the saintly qualities of the individual founder, but rather the communal practice of charisms that the organization stands for.[83]

Before moving on to contextualize structures of grace in the realm of business, it is important to reiterate that the work of describing and enacting these structures is a continuous process. This is similar to the disruption theory mentioned in the introduction. Remember Jenkins's illustration of the work as well of articulating and enforcing human rights where "the universal authority of human rights rests not in a shared ontology but in the continued performance of social practices that keep producing a [provisional and contested] vision of human dignity." The work of articulating and enacting structures of grace is also tied to the continuing work of

---

82. Ahern, *Structures of Grace*, 72.
83. Ahern, *Structures of Grace*, 72.

An Ethic of Disruption Towards Structures of Grace

identifying circumstances or conditions in which structures of grace are made insecure, or in which structures of sin continue to develop.[84]

THE BUSINESS VALUE CHAIN AND BUSINESS MODEL AS A STRUCTURE OF GRACE

We now further consider structures of grace specifically in the sphere of business. Because a structure of grace in business may take many different forms depending on the business's particular model or context, we will focus on something all businesses have in common—the business value chain—and the ways in which the business value chain can be shaped to function as a structure of grace.

The Business Value Chain and Business Model

The "business value chain" or network refers to a basic framework for illustrating and understanding the various aspects of a business and how they contribute to producing value for stakeholders. Michael Porter, known for his work in business strategy and economics, describes the outcome of the value chain as "the total revenues minus total costs of all activities undertaken to develop and market a product or service."[85] The value chain describes the different departments found in a business, their functions, and how the different departments contribute to the vision and mission of the business through their activities.

There are two main kinds of activities: the primary activities and the support activities. Primary activities include inbound logistics, operations, outbound logistics, marketing and sales, and after sales service. *Inbound logistics* are concerned with receiving inputs such as raw materials from suppliers. *Operations* relate to transforming these raw materials to the product or service that is of value to the customer. *Outbound logistics* entail delivering the product or service to the customer in a smooth and timely fashion. *Marketing and sales* promote the product or service to possible customers, communicating to them the presence of the business and the value it might offer to them. Lastly, *after sales service* maintains the relationship,

---

84. Jenkins, *Future of Ethics*, 118–19.
85. David and David, *Strategic Management*, 201.

the business has with its customers as well as the value of the product or service for them.

Under support activities, business have firm infrastructure, human resources, and technology development. *Firm infrastructure* includes departments and activities that provide support for the business's daily operations, such as legal or accounting and finance. *Human resources* functions to ensure that the people working in the business are treated and compensated properly, motivated, and trained for their respective roles in the organization. *Technology development* includes activities that relate to maintaining and procuring valuable information for the company, such as research and development or technological investment.

Recent work by entrepreneur Alex Osterwalder further distills the business value chain by highlighting the important aspects of the value chain for a particular product or service, using what he calls the business model canvas. The business value chain was originally constructed primarily with the linear operations of the manufacturing industry in mind. This is not necessarily the same model that is used today, particularly within the service industry and those that rely on digital platforms. Instead of the functions above, Osterwalder describes the business model as composed of nine building blocks: (1) customer segments; (2) value propositions of the business; (3) channels to deliver said value propositions; (4) customer relationships; (5) revenue streams; (6) key resources; (7) key activities; (8) key partnerships; and (9) cost structure.[86]

This business model canvas aims to streamline the description of a company's value chain development, especially in today's context where outsourcing certain parts of the value chain is common. In today's world, producing value is not necessarily measured in terms of concrete inputs and outputs, due to the certain industries, such as those in more technologically oriented or service-oriented fields, offering goods and services that are not as clearly defined or described as manufactured products.

Creating Shared Value

Through the value chain or business model, a business can "Create Shared Value," a term Porter uses to describe the way businesses should run. This works by generating not only financial returns for the business, but also addressing social issues in ways that may serve what Catholic social thought

---

86. Osterwalder and Pigneur, *Business Model Generation*, 16–17.

calls the common good.[87] For Porter and Kramer, creating shared value "will drive the next wave of innovation and productivity growth in the global economy" while also "reshap[ing] capitalism and its relationship to society."[88]

This concept of "Creating Shared Value" is used by many large companies—for example, Nestlé—as part of their corporate strategies and when articulating their vision and mission. An example of Nestlé's work in creating shared value is its emphasis on integrating suppliers such as small farms into the supply chain. Eliminating the middle person and investing in these small farms within the value chain ensures that Nestlé can consistently ensure a more quality product for customers. This also means compensation goes directly to those who are truly creating value, in this case, the farmers who grew the crops for the products. Nestlé and partners, the customer, and the suppliers all benefit.

Of course, the idea of a business helping address the needs of a community is not new, as business was originally part of the traditional economy, where addressing people's needs through the efficient exchange of goods and services was the main goal. However, in our complex modern business context, creating shared value can be difficult because often there is no easy "win-win" solution that can immediately and ethically address all stakeholders' needs. The concept of "Creating Shared Value" thus directs business owners and managers to be conscious of opportunities where the business might be able to create products and services that address social challenges and issues.

However, in order to implement the concept of creating shared value, businesses also need guidance through ethical frameworks and principles. For business academics Gaston de los Reyes, Markus Scholz, and N. Craig Smith, it is important to have norm-taking and norm-making frameworks in order to make the concept of creating shared value more robust and applicable for business owners and managers who are confronted with different managerial issues.[89] De los Reyes, Scholz, and Smith calls this position CSV+ (Creating Shared Value Plus), which entails using the concept of creating shared value, but also takes into account what moral norms can apply to the issue (norm-taking). Should the existing norms be insufficient for the current case, there must be a way to make the norms (norm-making)

---

87. Porter and Kramer, "Creating Shared Value."
88. Porter and Kramer, "Creating Shared Value."
89. Reyes et al., "Beyond the 'Win-Win,'" 142–67.

by helping business owners and managers "*identify* legitimate norms, and second, *prescribe* what to do when managers identify an applicable norm."[90]

Creating a business value chain that is also a structure of grace as well as a current business disruptor requires having a business abide by particular principles and practices that are norm-taking and norm-making. This is what's needed in order to holistically create shared value when confronted with the variety of cases with which owners and managers regularly deal with. There are three important principles that businesses must adopt to move towards being structures of grace and seek to create shared value must practice in their operations.

Principles Guiding a "Structure of Grace"-Oriented Business[91]

Principle One: Vision, Mission, and Strategy Are Tied to Stakeholders' Well-Being and the Common Good.

First, when businesses aim to disrupt their industries, their goals would be aligned with the well-being of individuals and the common good of the community. The Catholic social principle of the common good connects individual and communal flourishing as two vital components of the good towards which society should be striving. The common good thus includes the conditions necessary for individuals to holistically develop. In any given community, the common good must include all, and not just a select few. This understanding of the common good, and the overall vision of Catholic social thought, can help guide the process of design thinking in business

---

90. Reyes et al., "Beyond the 'Win-Win,'" 150–52.

91. Business ethics and theological ethics use the term "principle" differently. Business ethicists tend to use it broadly to define organizing tenets and best practices that help businesses grow and succeed, usually prescribed by top management as part of the business culture. While they are meant to be foundational, these principles can be changed quickly, often as businesses adapt the current buzzwords in their business strategy. Theological ethicists, on the other hand, would highlight that principles are ethical criteria for guiding and evaluating action and are to some degree enduring. In this case, principles seek to help guide moral decision-making: an example in Catholic ethics is the principle of double effect, which attempts to evaluate the permissibility of certain harmful actions. In this book, the term principle is used broadly to mean a normative organizing rule or code of conduct. Principles are something that an organization assumes as foundational to its operations and are directives that guide its projects and policies. Principles also serves as ethical criteria for the business, and are meant to be long-lasting in sustaining the business organization not just in terms of growth and traditional metrics for business success, but also in terms of the moral and ethical responsibilities placed on a business.

An Ethic of Disruption Towards Structures of Grace

decision-making by offering a redefinition of the business's goals and operations. The design thinking process, when guided by the common good, can help generate creative ideas on how businesses can create more just workplaces, and offer more ethical and accessible products and services. This will help them move towards becoming structures that promote dignity by making ethical choices and behavior more possible and accessible.

For a business guided by the common good, profit becomes the means towards flourishing rather than the end goal itself. Redirecting the business vision and mission towards well-being and the common good means taking a more long-term qualitative look at where the business is going, alongside the short-term quantitative profit motive. A business vision and mission grounded in the common good and human dignity dovetails with the concepts of creating shared value and CSV+ that business ethicists also advocate. It offers a good starting point for conversation about what a vision and mission grounded in creating shared value for the common good would look like for a particular organization.

Since a structure of grace is characterized by a continuous iteration and work for the flourishing of both human beings and the wider created world, it is important that the guiding vision, mission, and business strategy to become a beneficent structure are all crafted to be connected with the common good, through, for example, the creating shared value framework. When such a business reflects on its goals and direction, its focus will not simply be on offering particular products quickly or being "the best" in a particular industry, but also on situating these products and services within wider society. How would being the "best" in an industry help people or a community? How would satisfying a particular need improve a person's or a community's life? How would immediately bringing a product or service to the market and breaking a particular system help build new alternatives that would improve the welfare of people and the environment?

Because of the hierarchical organization present in many businesses, it is often the members of the management team, who are part of the firm's infrastructure, who have the decision-making power concerning business strategy and direction. Thus, the people who hold more power and directly shape and articulate the business's strategy and direction, need to be able to connect the firm's identity and operations to the bigger picture of the community the business is situated within and how their work contributes to the community's well-being.

The Ethics of Disruption in Business

Principle Two: There Is Effective Use of Conflict and Risk Management Using Innovation and Creativity, Grounded in the First Principle.

In the principles of design thinking, conflict and risk management are important parts of the process of addressing wicked problems and structures of sin. These are inevitable when current systems and structures are critiqued and interrupted. They are important because of the complicating presence of conflict and risk that manifest in wicked problems and structures of sin that businesses can and hopefully should disrupt. Given the limitations and constraints businesses deal with in today's complex and volatile socioeconomic and political settings, businesses that take their work seriously to become more like structures of grace will seek tools and best practices for managing these limitations, conflicting goods, and risks in a just and equitable way. They especially seek to disrupt the status quo and challenge bigger companies than themselves. This toolbox for handling conflict can also reveal ways that conflict can be a grace, by assisting organizations in identifying "particular occasions and broader patterns of life in which interests, desires, identities, and rights of individuals and groups are not being perceived, recognized, and respected by others."[92] As theologian Bradford Hinze argues, "the offer of God's grace can elicit an examination of conscience and a repudiation of prejudice and behavior that provide the conditions for conversion and transformation, repentance and healing."[93]

Proper conflict and risk management in a business working towards becoming a structure of grace will entail three things. First, it will take into account risks using accurate forms or risk management that do not over- or underestimate external opportunities and factors. While it can be tempting to see, for example, the enormous financial gains that a project might yield as sufficient incentive to execute that project, especially if the business is still establishing its presence in the market, the risks, and who would be shouldering those risks, must also be considered carefully. Second, the business's strategy should also account for long-term and short-term gains and losses and offer compromise among all the different stakeholders that do not overly burden or overly privilege any single stakeholder. This would entail, for example, a more thorough and expanded form of cost-benefit and multi-stakeholder analysis to determine the resources are needed for a project, both quantitative and qualitative advantages from the project, and

---

92. Hinze, "Grace of Conflict," 42.
93. Hinze, "Grace of Conflict," 42.

who would stand to gain or lose from the project. On the one hand, the business would have to establish the minimum rate of return required in order to ensure that the business and its workers are fairly compensated. On the other hand, if it is earning a very high financial return on a project, the business owners and managers might also reflect on whether their prices are fair to the client, or if there are ways to ensure that excess returns can be used to pursue other opportunities, either within the business or with other partner businesses or organizations that will benefit the common good.

Finally, when analyzing risks and losses, the projected risks and losses should not be unduly burdensome for only one or a few groups of people, and ideally should be shouldered according to the ability to absorb them. For instance, there may be cases where a start-up business cannot yet pay its workers, who are key suppliers, a living wage. While this might need to happen for the short-term, it would not be just if it were only the workers who are taking on this risk, and thus subsidizing the business by accepting the pay cut. The business owners can—and ought to—also shoulder this risk by limiting their own paychecks, for instance, and prioritizing plans that would enable the business to pay employees a living wage within a set amount of time and being clear about this plan and timeline with the business's workers.

Principle Three: The Business Practices Ongoing, Value-Focused Evaluation and Iteration, Grounded in the First and Second Principles.

A structure of grace is characterized by continuous work and improvement. A business with a structure of grace will practice ongoing, value-focused evaluation and iteration in order to improve their systems and processes as they innovate and change current systems, cultures, and structures. Design thinking's understanding of wicked problems can contribute to Catholic social thought's understanding of structures of sin. This understanding of structures of sin can greatly help in the iteration and evaluation. They can accurately identify and describe the structures that need to be renovated or replaced as the first step to generating solutions and iterating towards systems and processes that genuinely contribute to the common good.

Evaluation is important for critical self-appraisal in strategic management for smaller businesses to keep their unique selling propositions and advantages as they grow and push against other dominant market players to disrupt the system. It is also important in iterating towards becoming structures of grace in the face of new contexts and issues that may arise. Evaluation helps common good-oriented businesses continuously work towards this inclusive flourishing by measuring whether or not a business is reaching its vision and mission, grounded in the first principle, and guided by the considerations in the second principle above. To do this, business owners and managers must create a performance management system that does not just focus on the financials or quantifiable factors but seek to genuinely capture how the business is impacting lives, communities, and the ecosystem.

In the current global capitalist system, the predominant way of measuring what "good business" looks like is still to use the traditional indicator of quantitative growth—the growth of one's market share, the growth of one's stock price, or the growth of one's profit. This way of measuring business and economy is only indirectly connected to the way common good-oriented businesses would describe their mission—genuinely wanting to advance the well-being of the customer or society when they offer their products or services. While an increase in profits, for example, would to some extent reflect the care customers receive given the demand for the company's product or service, high demand alone may not necessarily reflect the degree of care and well-being needed not just by the customers, but by the employees, the local community, or the environment. Similarly, the growth of net profit or market share may be correlated with—but would not for certain show—whether care was adequately received by customers and other stakeholders, such as the environment.[94]

In relation to this, even when businesses strive to become more sustainable, if their success is judged primarily through financial indicators, these financial indicators will tend to take precedence, especially for investors who have the resources to fund their ventures. If businesses say that they want to engage in corporate social responsibility (CSR) or more responsible, sustainable, and inclusive business practices, the way stakeholders and shareholders evaluate the business should also be according to those standards, and not focus on growth and profit alone. Otherwise, the current status quo prevails.

As suggested above, a key part of effective evaluation is choosing the criteria to use to measure whether a common good-oriented business is reaching its goals for communal well-being and not just for profit. In the contemporary business world, one alternative set of metrics that dovetails

---

94. See Daly, *Beyond Growth*, 1.

with Catholic social thought's understanding of development and good business is issued by the governing body of what are known as B Corporations. B Corporations are businesses that commit themselves to doing business not just for the sake of profit for owners, but also for the good of all relevant stakeholders, by tackling a particular social or environmental problem or need through their business. B Corporation metrics are created and revised by the group of experts in business and academia, with feedback from various groups and users themselves. A company is assessed based on its location, industry, size, and so on, and these metrics seek to make it easier for investors and other users of financial information to compare and make sense of impact assessment data across businesses in a particular industry.

B Corporations focus on five areas of impact: governance, workers, community, environment, and customers. These five areas help investors "evaluate whether the company has either increased or decreased its emissions relative to the company's revenues or relative to the practices of other businesses, because this distinction helps a growing number of consumers, investors, and institutions who want to support businesses who put their values into action."[95] Their evaluations also rely on other data such as those from the Global Reporting Initiative (GRI) and Impact Reporting and Investment Standards (IRIS), organizations which B Corporations look to for best practices in impact reporting. B corporations aim to use the data to make it easier for consumers and investors to compare how well businesses are doing in terms of their impact on sustainability and on their communities. IRIS seeks to offer best practices in terms of how to measure such impact, as well as matches and develops metrics in line with the Sustainable Development Goals (SDGs) developed by the United Nations.

Another example of alternative evaluation tools is sustainability accounting. Overseen by the International Sustainability Standards Board (ISSB) of the International Financial Reporting Standards (IFRS) Foundation, sustainability accounting is a way that businesses can articulate relevant information about their businesses that is related to sustainability in ways that is helpful for business' various stakeholders, particularly in terms of the risks and opportunities present in the particular company and industry.[96] Businesses that employ this way of accounting hold themselves

---

95. B Lab, "Frequently Asked Questions."
96. Sustainability Accounting Standards Board, "About Us."

to standards that articulate the financial impact of sustainability and, based on that, the opportunities and risks for the stakeholders of the business.

In order to help businesses apply these principles as consistently as possible, evaluation and its results must be an important part of their business cycle and strategic planning, to monitor the progress and direction of the business, and the kind of alternative business it offers. As noted above, a key issue in such evaluations concerns the choice of metrics used. Mainstream business practices tend to focus mostly on quantitative and financial indicators, which reveals helpful information to keep the business going, but do not adequately capture whether or not a business is working towards flourishing and authentic development. For businesses concerned with creating alternative ways of doing business towards the common good, this leads to the question of what kind of indicators, when used together with quantitative and financial indicators, could offer a more robust and holistic picture of how the business affects not just the financial stakeholders of the company, but also other human beings, communities, and the environment, both in the short and long term.

CONCLUSION: ETHICAL DISRUPTION USING DESIGN THINKING AND CATHOLIC SOCIAL THOUGHT

For business people trying to improve their companies by making them more ethical, more sustainable, or more just, understanding the business value chain or model as a potential structure of grace might help generate new and more targeted ideas towards a better business in terms of the different functions and operations of the business. This is all done while challenging the already bigger businesses and disrupting the status quo. While the specific details will vary across different experiences, company sizes, and business models, certain key principles and practices can still be starting points for disrupting structures of sin and move towards structures of grace.

Operationalizing ethical disruption requires articulating guiding principles and questions that businesses can use in their own unique contexts. It also entails exploring and highlighting various case studies and models as illustrations to see the possibilities of what businesses can do. Businesses such as those in the Economy of Communion, for example, offer examples of businesses that seek to be structures of grace navigate the complexities of the business landscape today, how they discern what to do

An Ethic of Disruption Towards Structures of Grace

in the face of complex ethical situations, and challenging the way things are done. They also offer an alternative way of doing business, which, while not as disruptive as Facebook, Google, or Uber in terms of scale or noise, have nevertheless ethically disrupted their contexts and changed their local communities for the better, as seen in their stories.

The challenge of implementation and the question of scale is one that businesses will need to confront, given the questions of growth as well as impact raised in this chapter. Businesses at all levels will have to manage these two variables over the short and long term, given the need to care for all the stakeholders involved in the value chain, including the environment. As businesses grow, they will continue to find themselves in situations that present them with opportunities to disrupt the status quo for better or for worse. As organizations discern what to do in the face of these situations, the principles above can help them flesh out what to do and how they might chart a way forward.

Conclusion: Disrupting Structures and Moving Forward

BUSINESS PEOPLE ARE CONCERNED about viability, and often the concern is that, given limited resources, efforts to remain viable and efforts to adhere to ethical business practices will become a zero-sum game. Thus, executives may fear—or be convinced that—paying living wages might bankrupt the business, or caring for the environment will mean losing customers or profit. However, as seen in our case studies, there are ways of using limited resources creatively and equitably; but doing so entails thinking deeply about the interconnected issues and values involved, and a willingness to risk. When a company pursues this path, the first solutions generated in the process of iteration will likely not grant all stakeholders every one of their legitimates. The challenge for a business committed to the goal of becoming a structure for the common good, or a structure of grace, is to persist in seeking creative and effective ways to balance and equitably address the different concerns at stake. To do so, such businesses must keep in view all these needs both in the short and long term, while also being flexible and nimble in responding to and adjudicating conflicts among stakeholders as they arise.

Putting these four principles into practice is a daunting task, and one aspect of this challenge is to sustainably commit to the principles over the long term. Matters of fair working conditions and environmental sustainability are long-term goals that require continued iteration and work, and so necessitate further reflection on the resources that Catholic social thought and design thinking can offer in helping encourage and sustain businesses dedicated to becoming structures of grace over the long term.

Religion and theology are not always welcome nor included in discussions concerning business, business ethics, or innovation and disruption.

Part of this hesitation is the perception that religions bring with them an attitude of exclusivity against those who do not share the same faith or theology. The differences in language and concepts between the two disciplines can also serve as a barrier. Rather than be deterred, however, I have sought to bridge these gaps by using the language of design thinking—a concept understood and used by business practitioners—as a way to bring Catholic social thought in dialogue with business that is understandable to business people, and drives the conversation in business ethics forward towards a form of disruption.

In business ethics—particularly Christian business ethics—there can sometimes be a tendency to focus on individual action and how one can practice ethical behavior despite organizational culture or systems that might encourage otherwise. This approach to business ethics empowers individual decision-making and promotes discernment in order to navigate the complexities of the business world. Recent strands of business ethics, however, have also turned to larger business cultures and systems. While there have been efforts to focus on systems thinking and stakeholder theory in business, more work still needs to be done to address the very transformation of the systems and processes of business itself, plus the alternatives available people can use to imagine a different way of doing business. This involves both addressing the actions and behavior of individual moral agents, and understanding the structures within which business people work as well as the ways in which such structures affect business decision-making, amplifying the positive or negative effects of such decisions.[1] However, as John Paul II emphasized in his exposition on social sin in the documents during his papacy, human choices can either encourage or hinder the systems and structures within which human beings are embedded. Naming which choices—and whose choices—influence these systems and structures is crucial in understanding what elements need to be changed. Behavioral economics is an example of a discipline that examines how these individual choices are made—a discipline that incorporates psychology with economics. Rather than simply assuming that all human beings are rational agents who will make the same decision given a particular choice, behavioral economics explores the different "irrational"—or other than purely rational—choices that human beings also make. How these insights relate to both moral architecture and markets would be important

---

1. See Werhane, "Globalization, Mental Models, and Decentering Stakeholder Approaches," 129; Werhane, "Moral Imagination and Systems Thinking," 33–42.

Conclusion: Disrupting Structures and Moving Forward

to consider, given that the individual choices that aggregate over time will have profound effects on the kinds of systems and structures that are reinforced or taken down.

Acknowledging the persistence of profitability as an overriding motive for businesses and business people, while this dissertation has focused on structures, it nevertheless acknowledges the importance of what some might call "political will" to actually implement the recommendations and ideas that are suggested. In summoning this political will, ethical business leadership is key, but all employees have a role to play. Gentile, Meyerson, and several others focus on individual employees' choices and how to go "against the grain" and practice their own values amidst opposing forces.[2] This practice and courage are even more vital at the top levels where senior business leaders have more decision-making power and a bigger circle of influence. When decisions are made at these highest management levels, more people are affected, and thus questions of influence, consequences, and implications of decisions made become more complex and more difficult to account for. At the same time, people at this level are faced with more pressure from stakeholders, particularly shareholders with money invested into the business, and often have less time to gather enough resources to make an informed decision.

My work seeks to connect design thinking and Catholic social thought to create a possible approach for pursuing much-needed systemic change in business towards an ethical form of disruption towards the common good. Design thinking and Catholic social thought offer insights that can complement each other's strengths and address each other's weaknesses. This dialogue between design thinking and Catholic social thought offers principles that business persons can use when navigating complex business structures, systems, and processes. The dialogue is also a fruitful space for innovating business practice by facilitating encounter between various disciplines that is inclusive, manages conflict productively, and welcomes creativity. This manner can be cultivated to help business people practice ethical business leadership and decision-making in their own particular organizations—what scholars call "adaptive leadership"—rather than just quick technical fixes where solutions are pre-determined.[3]

---

2. See Gentile, *Giving Voice to Values*; Meyerson, *Tempered Radicals*, for examples of work that discusses how a worker can practice their agency and values, as well as effect change in their particular workplaces.

3. See Heifetz et al., *Practice of Adaptive Leadership*.

The Ethics of Disruption in Business

These considerations on individual as well as structural aspects of the business point to the need for further attention to the question of ethical business leadership. While it is dismissed by some as an often-overused buzzword, forming ethical business leadership is an important task that entails cultivating the knowledge, skills, and virtues needed to lead an organization well, and with a concern for the common good, even as a small business challenging its bigger contemporaries. Towards this end, ethical business practice calls for developing the virtue of prudence or practical wisdom, terms not always used in business literature but certainly implied in the way ethics-minded practitioners talk about how decisions are made.[4] Danya Ruttenberg, an American rabbi and scholar, movingly expresses this concern for practical wisdom among today's business community:

> We need leadership that is brave and bold and that holds the pain and fear that people are feeling and helps them to see a vision of what's possible that is new, that is the change that is needed—that is not clinging to a past that will never again be. How can we hold each other in this space of unknowns? What do we need to do to let go of who we have been so that we can become who we still yet can be? How can we make our decisions about our future from a place of vision, not fear? *Even if we don't have all the answers now, even if there are some answers that can not yet be known, how can we use the ways in which this time invites us to expand our understanding of what's possible?*[5]

Design thinking informed by Catholic social thought encourages the kind of leadership Ruttenberg describes and raises the same kinds of questions. The last sentence above is an especially important question to ask, given the many unknowns to face and the many assumptions to make—assumptions that may need to change quickly in fast-moving, complex situations. While Catholic social thought can offer insights into the vision needed, the way business leaders are formed, both in their families and in their educations, and also by the extant cultures of business and companies, it is also crucial in inculcating genuine care for the common good and ethical business leadership, rather than a focus on image-building or profits alone.

---

4. Wittmer, *Developing Practical Wisdom in Ethical Decision Making*, 169–83.

5. Ruttenberg, "Let's Talk about Trauma, Terror, and the Golden Calf for a Moment, Shall We?" Emphasis added.

Conclusion: Disrupting Structures and Moving Forward

Reimagining and innovating business systems and processes does not happen overnight, nor is it a one-time event. It is a continuous and dynamic process that challenges business people to balance the needs of all stakeholders involved as businesses and their externalities evolve, given limited resources. As companies continue to evolve in the face a complex world, the principles outlined in this book are an important reminder and guide for businesses when navigating the ethical aspect of their operations and trying to disrupt the ways in which business is done as a smaller entity that might not have as much power yet.

With the further challenges and questions raised, design thinking practitioners will also continue to iterate the design thinking process, and consider other concepts such as the Creativity Quotient that Bruce Nussbaum, a professor of innovation and design at Parsons the New School of Design, advocates for in his work that challenges design thinking.[6] Theologians also continue to develop and deepen Catholic social thought in response to the "signs of the times."[7] Given the iterations happening in both disciplines, the conversation between the two also continue and deepen as a helpful resource for business people in the future.

---

6. Nussbaum, "Design Thinking Is A Failed Experiment."
7. Second Vatican Council, *Gaudium et Spes*, sec. 4.

Bibliography

Abesamis, Carlos H. *A Third Look at Jesus.* 3rd ed. Quezon City: Claretian, 1999.

Ahern, Kevin. *Structures of Grace: Catholic Organizations Serving the Global Common Good.* Maryknoll, NY: Orbis, 2015.

Aldrich, John H. *Interdisciplinarity: Its Role in a Discipline Based Academy.* New York: Oxford University Press, 2014.

Aquinas, Thomas. *Summa Theologica.* Translated by Fathers of the English Dominican Province. New York: Benziger Brothers, 2017. https://www.newadvent.org/summa/.

Badenhausen, Kurt. "The World's Most Valuable Brands 2018." *Forbes,* May 23, 2018. https://www.forbes.com/sites/kurtbadenhausen/2018/05/23/the-worlds-most-valuable-brands-2018/.

Badiou, Alain, and Marcel Gauchet. *What Is to be Done? A Dialogue on Communism, Capitalism, and the Future of Democracy.* Translated by Susan Spitzer. Malden, MA: Polity, 2016.

Barrera, Albino. *Economic Compulsion and Christian Ethics.* New York: Cambridge University, 2007.

———. *Market Complicity and Christian Ethics.* New York: Cambridge University, 2011.

Bauckham, Richard. *The Bible and Ecology: Rediscovering the Community of Creation.* Waco, TX.: Baylor University, 2010.

Baum, Gregory. *Religion and Alienation: A Theological Reading of Sociology.* Maryknoll, NY: Orbis, 1975.

Baxter, Will. "Boosting Resilience and Independence in Kenya." *Catholic Relief Services,* November 11, 2019. https://www.crs.org/stories/boosting-resilience-and-independence-kenya.

B Corporations Impact Assessment. "B Impact Assessment—Measure What Matters Most." https://bimpactassessment.net/.

Beaton, Richard, and Linda Wagener. "Building Healthy Organizations in Which People Can Flourish." In *Beyond Integrity: A Judeo-Christian Approach to Business Ethics,* 279–85. 3rd ed. Grand Rapids: Zondervan, 2012.

Bellissimo-Magrin, Maria. "How the Disruptive Uber Business Model Is Changing the Way Business Owners Think." *Dynamic Business,* May 8, 2018. https://dynamicbusiness.com/topics/small-business-resources/social-media-strategy-social-media/how-the-disruptive-uber-business-model-is-changing-the-way-business-owners-think.html.

Benedict XVI. *On Christian Hope: Spe Salvi.* http://www.vatican.va/content/benedict-xvi/en/encyclicals/documents/hf_ben-xvi_enc_20071130_spe-salvi.html.

Bibliography

———. *On Integral Human Development in Charity and Truth: Caritas in Veritate*. http://w2.vatican.va/content/benedict-xvi/en/encyclicals/documents/hf_ben-xvi_enc_20090629_caritas-in-veritate.html.

Berger, Peter L., and Thomas Luckmann. *The Social Construction of Reality: A Treatise in the Sociology of Knowledge*. Garden City, NY: Doubleday, 1967.

Berry, John Anthony. "What Makes Us Human? Augustine on Interiority, Exteriority, and the Self." *Scientia et Fides* 5 (2017) 87–106.

Birch, Bruce C. *What Does the Lord Require? The Old Testament Call to Social Witness*. Louisville, KY: Westminster John Knox, 1985.

B Lab. "Frequently Asked Questions." *B Corporations Impact Assessment*. https://bimpactassessment.net/how-it-works/frequently-asked-questions/top-10.

Blair, Ryan. "5 Steps of Compartmentalization: The Secret Behind Successful Entrepreneurs." *Forbes*, June 26, 2012. https://www.forbes.com/sites/ryanblair/2012/06/26/5-steps-of-compartmentalization/.

Blount, Sally. "Yes, the World Needs More MBAs. Here's Why." *Bloomberg*, May 13, 2014. https://www.bloomberg.com/news/articles/2014-05-13/yes-the-world-needs-more-mbas-dot-here-s-why.

Boff, Leonardo. *Church: Charism and Power*. New York: Crossroad, 1985.

Bordoni, Linda. "Pope Francis: 'Death Penalty Inadmissable.'" *Vatican News*, August 2, 2018. https://www.vaticannews.va/en/pope/news/2018-08/pope-francis-cdf-ccc-death-penalty-revision-ladaria.html.

Bowles, Samuel, and Herbert Gintis. *A Cooperative Species: Human Reciprocity and Its Evolution*. Princeton: Princeton University, 2011.

Boyd, Colin. "The Nestlé Infant Formula Controversy and a Strange Web of Subsequent Business Scandals." *Journal of Business Ethics* 106 (2011) 283–93.

Brady, Bernard V. *Essential Catholic Social Thought*. 2nd ed. Maryknoll, NY: Orbis, 2017.

Brecht, Mara. "See–Judge . . . Act? The Role of Action in the Anti-Racist Catholic Theological Classroom." *Religious Education* 114 (2019) 202–13.

Brown, Tim. *Change by Design: How Design Thinking Transforms Organizations and Inspires Innovation*. Rev. ed. New York: Harper Business, 2019.

Buckeye, Jeanne G., et al. "Mundell and Associates, Inc.: Managing When Faith Really Matters." *Case Research Journal* 31 (2011) 1–15.

Bulaong, Oscar, Jr. "Explicitly Integrating Systemic/Institutional Thinking in Business Ethics Education." In *Business Ethics in Asia: Issues and Cases*, edited by Oscar Bulaong Jr. et al., 15–21. Quezon City: Ateneo de Manila University, 2014.

Burke, Margaret Ellen. "Social Sin and Social Grace." *The Way Supplement* 85 (1996) 40–54.

Canning, Anna. "Small Scale Farmers Stand Up to Nestlé Coffee Processing Plant." *Fair World Project*, January 31, 2019. https://fairworldproject.org/small-scale-coffee-farmers-stand-up-to-Nestlé/.

Capps C. F. "Formal and Material Cooperation with Evil." *American Catholic Philosophical Quarterly* 89 (2015) 681–98.

Carroll, John J. "Social Theory and Social Change in the Philippines." *Pulso (Institute on Church and Social Issues)* 1 (1984) 34–47.

Case, Mary Ann. "The Role of the Popes in the Invention of Complementarity and the Vatican's Anathematization of Gender." *Religion and Gender* 6 (2016) 155–72.

Castillo, Daniel P. *An Ecological Theology of Liberation: Salvation and Political Ecology*. Maryknoll, NY: Orbis, 2019.

Bibliography

Cavanaugh, William T. *Being Consumed: Economics and Christian Desire.* Grand Rapids: Eerdmans, 2008.

Christensen, Clayton M. *The Innovators' Dilemma: When New Technologies Cause Great Firms to Fail.* Reprint ed. Boston: Harvard Business Review Press, 2016.

Christensen, Clayton M., et al. "What Is Disruptive Innovation?" *Harvard Business Review,* December 2015. https://hbr.org/2015/12/what-is-disruptive-innovation.

Churchman, C. West. "Guest Editorial: Wicked Problems." *Management Science* 14 (1967) 141–42.

Clark, Meghan J. "Caritas in Veritate." In *Modern Catholic Social Teaching: Commentaries and Interpretations,* edited by Kenneth Himes. 2nd ed. Washington, DC: Georgetown University Press, 2018.

———. *The Vision of Catholic Social Thought: The Virtue of Solidarity and the Praxis of Human Rights.* Minneapolis: Fortress, 2014.

Curran, Charles E. "Catholic Social and Sexual Teaching: A Methodological Comparison." *Theology Today* 44 (1988) 425–40.

———. *Catholic Social Teaching, 1891–Present: A Historical, Theological, and Ethical Analysis.* Washington, DC: Georgetown University Press, 2002.

———. "A Century of Catholic Social Teaching." *Theology Today* 48 (1991) 154–69.

Currie, Graeme, et al. "A Call for University-Based Business Schools to 'Lower Their Walls': Collaborating With Other Academic Departments in Pursuit of Social Value." *Academy of Management Learning and Education* 15 (2016) 742–55.

Daly, Daniel J. "Structures of Virtue and Vice." *New Blackfriars* 92 (2011) 341–57.

———. *The Structures of Virtue and Vice.* Washington, DC: Georgetown University Press, 2021.

Daly, Herman E. *Beyond Growth: The Economics of Sustainable Development.* Boston: Beacon, 1997.

David, Fred R., and Forest R. David. *Strategic Management: A Competitive Advantage Approach, Concepts, and Cases.* 16th ed. Essex: Pearson Education, 2017.

Davis, John Jefferson. "Economic Growth vs. the Environment? The Need for New Paradigms in Economics, Business Ethics, and Evangelical Theology." *Evangelical Review of Theology* 41 (2017) 57–66.

Devinney, Timothy M., et al. *The Myth of the Ethical Consumer.* New York: Cambridge University, 2010.

Dicastery for Promoting Integral Human Development. "Considerations for an Ethical Discernment Regarding Some Aspects of the Present Economic-Financial System: *Oeconomicae et Pecuniariae Quaestiones.*" https://.vaticanva/content/salastampa/en/bollettino/pubblico/2018/05/17/180517a.html.

———. "Vocation of the Business Leader: A Reflection." Dicastery for Promoting Integral Human Development and the John A. Ryan Institute for Catholic Social Thought of the Center for Catholic Studies at the University of St. Thomas, 2018. https://www.stthomas.edu/media/catholicstudies/center/ryan/publications/publicationpdfs/vocationofthebusinessleaderpdf/FinalTextTheVocationoftheBusinessLeader.pdf.

Doran, Robern. *Theology and the Dialectics of History.* 2nd ed. Toronto: University of Toronto Press, 1990.

Dorr, Donal. *Option for the Poor and for the Earth: Catholic Social Teaching.* 20th Anniversary ed. Maryknoll, NY: Orbis, 2012.

East Asian Pastoral Institute. "Structural Poverty—The Structures of Sin." http://www.eapi.org.ph/resources/eapr/east-asian-pastoral-review-1999/chapter-9-structural-poverty-the-structures-of-sin/.

Bibliography

Ellacuría, Ignacio. *Ignacio Ellacuría: Essays on History, Liberation, and Salvation.* Edited by Michael E. Lee. Maryknoll, NY: Orbis, 2013.

Ellacuría, Ignacio, and Jon Sobrino, eds. *Mysterium Liberationis: Fundamental Concepts of Liberation Theology.* Maryknoll, NY: Orbis, 1993.

Fair Trade International. "Fair Trade Standards." https://www.fairtrade.net/standard.

Federation of Asian Bishops' Conference–First Asian Institute for Social Action. "Becoming the Church of the Poor: With Industrial Workers." Federation of Asian Bishops Conferences, 1987.

Fernandez, Eleazar. *Reimagining the Human: Theological Anthropology in Response to Systemic Evil.* St. Louis: Chalice, 2004.

Finn, Daniel K., ed. *Distant Markets, Distant Harms: Economic Complicity and Christian Ethics.* New York: Oxford University, 2014.

———. *The Moral Ecology of Markets: Assessing Claims about Markets and Justice.* New York: Cambridge University, 2006.

———. "What Is a Sinful Social Structure?" *Theological Studies* 77 (2016) 136–64.

Francis. *Apostolic Exhortation on the Proclamation of the Gospel in Today's World: Evangelii Gaudium.* http://w2.vatican.va/content/francesco/en/apost_exhortations/documents/papa-francesco_esortazione-ap_20131124_evangelii-gaudium.html.

———. "Homily of Holy Father Francis: Visit to Lampedusa." http://www.vatican.va/content/francesco/en/homilies/2013/documents/papa-francesco_20130708_omelia-lampedusa.html.

———. *On Care for Our Common Home: Laudato Si'.* http://w2.vatican.va/content/francesco/en/encyclicals/documents/papa-francesco_20150524_enciclica-laudato-si.html.

———. *On Fraternity and Social Friendship: Fratelli Tutti.* http://www.vatican.va/content/francesco/en/encyclicals/documents/papa-francesco_20201003_enciclica-fratelli-tutti.html.

———. *On the Climate Crisis: Laudate Deum.* https://www.vatican.va/content/francesco/en/apost_exhortations/documents/20231004-laudate-deum.html.

———. "Pope Calls for a 'Listening Church.'" *America Magazine*, October 17, 2015. https://www.americamagazine.org/content/all-things/pope-calls-listening-church.

———. *Post-Synodal Exhortation to the People of God and to All Persons of Good Will: Querida Amazonia.* http://w2.vatican.va/content/francesco/en/apost_exhortations/documents/papa-francesco_esortazione-ap_20200202_querida-amazonia.html.

———. "To the Participants in the Plenary Assembly of the Dicastery for the Laity, the Family, and Life (November 16, 2019)." http://w2.vatican.va/content/francesco/it/speeches/2019/november/documents/papa-francesco_20191116_laici-famiglia-vita.html.

Francis, Diane M. "Facebook's Ethical Problem." *HuffPost*, September 25, 2017. https://www.huffpost.com/entry/face-ethical-problem_b_59c923f9e4b0b7022a646c61.

Gallagher, John, and Jeanne Buckeye. *Structures of Grace: The Business Practices of the Economy of Communion.* Hyde Park, NY: New City, 2014.

Garbagnoli, Sara. "Against the Heresy of Immanence: Vatican's 'Gender' as a New Rhetorical Device against the Denaturalization of the Sexual Order." *Religion and Gender* 6 (2016) 187–204.

Gee, Ted. *Hope Is Not a Strategy: Simple Solutions for Doing Business in the 21st Century.* Indianapolis: Dog Ear, 2008.

Bibliography

Gentile, Mary C. *Giving Voice to Values: How to Speak Your Mind When You Know What's Right.* New Haven, CT: Yale University Press, 2012.

Gleeson, Brent. "The Silo Mentality: How to Break Down the Barriers." *Forbes*, October 2, 2013. https://www.forbes.com/sites/brentgleeson/2013/10/02/the-silo-mentality-how-to-break-down-the-barriers/.

Goodman, Michael. "Systems Thinking: What, Why, When, Where, and How?" *The Systems Thinker*, February 27, 2016. https://thesystemsthinker.com/systems-thinking-what-why-when-where-and-how/.

Grenz, Stanley J. *The Social God and the Relational Self: A Trinitarian Theology of the Imago Dei.* Louisville, KY: Westminster John Knox, 2001.

Griffiths, Peter. "Lack of Rigour in Defending Fairtrade: A Rejoinder to Alistair Smith." *Economic Affairs* 31 (2011) 103–4.

Gutiérrez, Gustavo. *A Theology of Liberation: History, Politics, and Salvation.* Translated by Caridad Inda and John Eagleson. Rev. ed. Maryknoll, NY: Orbis, 1988.

Guttentag, Daniel. "Airbnb: Disruptive Innovation and the Rise of an Informal Tourism Accommodation Sector." *Current Issues in Tourism* 18 (2015) 1192–217.

Haigh, Nardia, and Andrew Griffiths. "The Natural Environment as Primary Stakeholder." *Business Strategy and the Environment* 18 (2009) 347–59.

Haight, Roger. *The Experience and Language of Grace.* New York: Paulist, 1979.

Hamrlik, Kathryn Reyes. "The Principle of Subsidiarity and Catholic Ecclesiology: Implications for the Laity." PhD diss., Loyola University Chicago, 2011.

Haslam, Molly C. *A Constructive Theology of Intellectual Disability: Human Being as Mutuality and Response.* New York: Fordham University Press, 2011.

Heifetz, Ronald A., et al. *The Practice of Adaptive Leadership: Tools and Tactics for Changing Your Organization and the World.* Boston: Harvard Business School Press, 2009.

Heyer, Kristin E. "Walls in the Heart: Social Sin in *Fratelli Tutti*." *Journal of Catholic Social Thought* 19 (2022) 25–40.

Himes, Kenneth R., ed. *Modern Catholic Social Teaching: Commentaries and Interpretations.* 2nd ed. Washington, DC: Georgetown University Press, 2018.

Hinze, Bradford. "The Grace of Conflict." *Theological Studies* 81 (2020) 40–64.

Hinze, Christine Firer. "Economic Recession, Work, and Solidarity." *Theological Studies* 72 (2011) 150–69.

———. *Radical Sufficiency: Work, Livelihood, and a US Catholic Economic Ethic.* Washington, DC: Georgetown University Press, 2021.

Hodson, Michael. "Design Thinking: The Missing Link between Theology and Business Practice?" *Faith in Business Quarterly Journal* 13 (2011) 23–25.

Hollenbach, David. *The Common Good and Christian Ethics.* New York: Cambridge University, 2002.

Hoover-Kinsinger, Sandra E. "Hoping against Hope: An Integration of the Hope Theology of Jurgen Moltmann and C. R. Snyder's Psychology of Hope." *Journal of Psychology and Christianity* 37 (2018) 313–22.

IDEO. *Field Guide to Human-Centered Design.* San Francisco: IDEO, 2015.

International Theological Commission. "Communion and Stewardship: Human Persons Created in the Image of God." http://www.vatican.va/roman_curia/congregations/cfaith/cti_documents/rc_con_cfaith_doc_20040723_communion-stewardship_en.html.

Bibliography

———. "In Search of a Universal Ethic: A New Look at the Natural Law." http://www.vatican.va/roman_curia/congregations/cfaith/cti_documents/rc_con_cfaith_doc_20090520_legge-naturale_en.html.

———. "*Sensus Fidei* in the Life of the Church." http://www.vatican.va/roman_curia/congregations/cfaith/cti_documents/rc_cti_20140610_sensus-fidei_en.html.

Iskander, Natasha. "Design Thinking Is Fundamentally Conservative and Preserves the Status Quo." *Harvard Business Review*, September 5, 2018. https://hbr.org/2018/09/design-thinking-is-fundamentally-conservative-and-preserves-the-status-quo.

Jacobs, Michael. "The Environment as Stakeholder." *Business Strategy Review* 8 (1997) 25–28.

Jarvis, Jonathan. "The Crisis of Credit Visualized." https://vimeo.com/3261363.

Jenkins, Willis. *The Future of Ethics: Sustainability, Social Justice, and Religious Creativity.* Washington, DC: Georgetown University Press, 2013.

John Paul II. *Apostolic Exhortation on Reconciliation and Penance: Reconciliatio et Paenitentia.* http://w2.vatican.va/content/john-paul-ii/en/apost_exhortations/documents/hf_jp-ii_exh_02121984_reconciliatio-et-paenitentia.html.

———. *On Human Work and on the Ninetieth Anniversary of Rerum Novarum: Laborem Exercens.* http://w2.vatican.va/content/john-paul-ii/en/encyclicals/documents/hf_jp-ii_enc_14091981_laborem-exercens.html.

———. *On the Hundredth Anniversary of Rerum Novarum: Centesimus Annus.* http://w2.vatican.va/content/john-paul-ii/en/encyclicals/documents/hf_jp-ii_enc_01051991_centesimus-annus.html.

———. *On the Twentieth Anniversary of Populorum Progressio: Sollicitudo Rei Socialis.* http://w2.vatican.va/content/john-paul-ii/en/encyclicals/documents/hf_jp-ii_enc_30121987_sollicitudo-rei-socialis.html.

John XXIII. *On Christianity and Social Progress: Mater et Magistra.* http://w2.vatican.va/content/john-xxiii/en/encyclicals/documents/hf_j-xxiii_enc_15051961_mater.html.

———. *On Establishing Universal Peace in Truth, Justice, Charity, and Liberty: Pacem in Terris.* http://w2.vatican.va/content/john-xxiii/en/encyclicals/documents/hf_j-xxiii_enc_11041963_pacem.html.

Johnson, Elizabeth. *Ask the Beasts: Darwin and the God of Love.* London: Bloomsbury, 2014.

———. "Spirit-Sophia." In *She Who Is: The Mystery of God in Feminist Theological Discourse*, 124–49. New York: Crossroad, 1997.

Keenan, James F. *A History of Catholic Moral Theology in the Twentieth Century: From Confessing Sins to Liberating Consciences.* New York: Continuum, 2010.

Kelly, Conor. "The Nature and Operation of Structural Sin: Additional Insights from Theology and Moral Psychology." *Theological Studies* 80 (2019) 293–327.

Kim, W. Chan, and Renée Mauborgne. *Beyond Disruption: Innovate and Achieve Growth without Displacing Industries, Companies, or Jobs.* Boston: Harvard Business Review Press, 2023.

Kolawole, Emi. "Design for Worldview: A New Way to Teach Design Thinking." *Stanford d.school blog*, August 31, 2016. https://medium.com/stanford-d-school/design-for-worldview-a-new-way-to-teach-design-thinking-a3478559e408.

Laczniak, Gene R. "Distributive Justice, Catholic Social Teaching, and the Moral Responsibility of Marketers." *Journal of Public Policy and Marketing* 18 (1999) 125–29.

Bibliography

Laczniak, Gene, et al. "On the Nature of 'Good' Goods and the Ethical Role of Marketing." *Journal of Catholic Social Thought* 13 (2016) 63–81.

Latin American Bishops Conference. "Medellin Conference 1968." Latin American Bishops Conference, September 6, 1968. http://www.laikos.org/medellin_conference_1968.htm.

Legaspi, Leonardo Z. "Looking Back, Looking Forward: Revisiting PCP II." In *The Second Plenary Council of the Philippines: Quo Vadis?*, edited by Eric Marcelo O. Genilo et al., 1–14. Quezon City: Ateneo de Manila University, 2015.

Leo XIII. *On Capital and Labor: Rerum Novarum*. http://w2.vatican.va/content/leo-xiii/en/encyclicals/documents/hf_l-xiii_enc_15051891_rerum-novarum.html.

Levin, Kelly, et al. "Overcoming the Tragedy of Super Wicked Problems." *Policy Sciences* 45 (2012) 123–52.

Liedtka, Jeanne, et al. *Design Thinking for the Greater Good: Innovation in the Social Sector*. New York: Columbia University Press, 2017.

Living Climate Change. "Living Climate Change—All about Climate Change." http://www.livingclimatechange.com/.

Lonergan, Bernard J. F. *Insight: A Study of Human Understanding*. Edited by Frederick E. Crowe and Robert M. Doran. 5th ed. Toronto: University of Toronto Press, 1992.

———. *Method in Theology*. Toronto: University of Toronto Press, 1990.

———. *A Second Collection: Volume 13*. Edited by Robert M. Doran and John Dadosky. 2nd ed. Collected Works of Bernard Lonergan. Toronto: University of Toronto Press, 2016.

Marcel, Gabriel. *Creative Fidelity*. Translated by Robert Rosthal. New York: Fordham University Press, 2002.

Marshall, Donna, et al. "Piggy in the Middle: How Direct Customer Power Affects First Tier Suppliers' Adoption of Socially Responsible Procurement Practices and Performance." *Journal of Business Ethics* 154 (2019) 1081–1102.

Martin, James. "Where Were the Voting Women at the Synod?" *America Magazine*, October 24, 2015. https://www.americamagazine.org/content/all-things/where-were-voting-women-synod-0.

Massingale, Bryan. *Racial Justice and the Catholic Church*. Maryknoll, NY: Orbis, 2010.

———. "The Scandal of Poverty: 'Cultured Indifference' and the Option for the Poor Post-Katrina." *Journal of Religion and Society Supplement Series* 4 (2008) 55–72.

Matthews, Joe. "The Sharing Economy Boom Is about to Bust." *TIME*, June 27, 2014. https://time.com/2924778/airbnb-uber-sharing-economy/.

Matulich, Erika, and Robert McMurrian. "Building Customer Value and Profitability with Business Ethics." *Journal of Business and Economic Research* 4 (2006) 11–18.

McArdle, Louise, and Pete Thomas. "Fair Enough? Women and Fair Trade." *Critical Perspectives on International Business* 8 (2012) 277–94.

McElwee, Joshua J. "Theologians Praise Pope's Historic Appointment of Women as Members of Vatican Congregation." *National Catholic Reporter*, July 11, 2019. https://www.ncronline.org/news/vatican/theologians-praise-popes-historic-appointment-women-members-vatican-congregation.

McEnroy, Carmel E. *Guests in Their Own House: The Women of Vatican II*. Eugene, OR: Wipf & Stock, 2011.

McIntyre, Alison. "Doctrine of Double Effect." In *The Stanford Encyclopedia of Philosophy*, edited by Edward N. Zalta and Uri Nodelman. https://plato.stanford.edu/archives/win2023/entries/double-effect/.

Bibliography

McRorie, Christina. "Markets as Moral Architectures." Conference Presentation presented at the Society of Christian Ethics Annual Meeting, Washington, DC, January 9, 2020.

Melchin, Kenneth R. *Living with Other People: An Introduction to Christian Ethics Based on Bernard Lonergan*. St. Paul University Series in Ethics. Collegeville, MN: Liturgical, 1998.

Melé, Domènec. "The Firm as a 'Community of Persons': A Pillar of Humanistic Business Ethos." *Journal of Business Ethics* 106 (2012) 89–101.

Melé, Domènec, and César González Cantón. "The *Homo Economicus* Model." In *Human Foundations of Management: Understanding the Homo Humanus*, edited by Domènec Melé and César González Cantón, 9–29. IESE Business Collection. London: Palgrave Macmillan UK, 2014.

Mendoza, René, and Johan Bastiaensen. "Fair Trade and the Coffee Crisis in the Nicaraguan Segovias." *Small Enterprise Development* 14 (2003) 36–46.

Meyerson, Debra E. *Tempered Radicals: How People Use Difference to Inspire Change at Work*. Boston: Harvard Business School Press, 2001.

Meyerson, Debra E., and Maureen A. Scully. "Tempered Radicalism and the Politics of Ambivalence and Change." *Organization Science* 6 (1995) 585–600.

Nam, Su-Jung, and Hyesun Hwang. "What Makes Consumers Respond to Creating Shared Value Strategy? Considering Consumers as Stakeholders in Sustainable Development." *Corporate Social Responsibility and Environmental Management* 26 (2019) 388–95.

Nash, James. *Loving Nature: Ecological Integrity and Christian Responsibility*. Nashville: Abingdon, 1991.

Naughton, Michael, et al. "Respect in Action: Applying Subsidiarity in Business." https://uniapac.org/wp-content/uploads/2019/11/Book-Respect-In-Action-ENG.pdf.

Naughton, Michael, and Gene R. Laczniak. "A Theological Context of Work from the Catholic Social Encyclical Tradition." *Journal of Business Ethics* 12 (1993) 981–94.

Nestlé, "Nestlé Supports Coffee, Sugar Farmers via Public-Private Partnerships." August 30, 2019. https://www.nestle.com.ph/media/news/coffee-sugar-farmers-support.

Nichols, Terence L. *That All May Be One: Hierarchy and Participation in the Church*. Collegeville, MN: Glazier, 1997.

Novak, Michael. *Toward a Theology of the Corporation*. Washington, DC: American Enterprise Institute for Public Policy Research, 1981.

Nussbaum, Bruce. "Design Thinking Is a Failed Experiment. So What's Next?" *Fast Company*, April 5, 2011. https://www.fastcompany.com/1663558/design-thinking-is-a-failed-experiment-so-whats-next.

O'Boyle, Edward, et al. "The GOOD Company." *Corporate Governance International Journal of Business in Society* 11 (2011) 1–19.

O'Keefe, Mark. *What Are They Saying about Social Sin?* New York: Paulist, 1990.

O'Loughlin, Michael J. "While Homosexuality Is Still Illegal, Pope Francis Has Thrown a Lifeline to LGBT Catholics." *America Magazine*, October 23, 2020. https://www.americamagazine.org/faith/2020/10/23/pope-francis-homosexuality-illegal-lgbt-catholics.

Ong, Jonathan Corpus, and Jason Vincent A. Cabanes. "Architects of Networked Disinformation: Behind the Scenes of Troll Accounts and Fake News Production in the Philippines." http://newtontechfordev.com/wp-content/uploads/2018/02/ARCHITECTS-OF-NETWORKED-DISINFORMATION-FULL-REPORT.pdf.

Osterwalder, Alexander, and Yves Pigneur. *Business Model Generation*. Hoboken, NJ: Wiley, 2010.

Bibliography

Overman, Steven. *The Conscience Economy: How a Mass Movement for Good Is Great for Business.* Brookline, MA: Bibliomotion, 2014.

Page, Rick. *Hope Is Not a Strategy: The 6 Keys to Winning the Complex Sale.* New York: McGraw-Hill Professional, 2003.

Papanek, Victor. *Design for the Real World: Human Ecology and Social Change.* Rev. ed. Chicago: Chicago Review, 2005.

Pasanen, Jussi. "Human Centred Design Considered Harmful." *Jussi Pasanen* (blog), January 28, 2019. https://www.jussipasanen.com/human-centred-design-considered-harmful/.

Paul VI. *Apostolic Letter of Pope Paul VI on the Occasion of the Eightieth Anniversary of the Encyclical Rerum Novarum: Octogesima Adveniens.* http://w2.vatican.va/content/paul-vi/en/apost_letters/documents/hf_p-vi_apl_19710514_octogesima-adveniens.html.

———. *On the Development of Peoples: Populorum Progressio.* http://w2.vatican.va/content/paul-vi/en/encyclicals/documents/hf_p-vi_enc_26031967_populorum.html.

Peterson, Hayley. "10 Companies That Control Almost Everything We Eat." *Business Insider,* July 7, 2014. https://www.businessinsider.com/10-companies-that-control-what-we-buy-2014-7.

Pilario, Daniel Franklin E. "Revisiting See-Judge-Act: Reflections from Asia." *Concilium* 1 (2016) 83–92.

Pirson, Michael. "A Humanistic Perspective for Management Theory: Protecting Dignity and Promoting Well-Being." *Journal of Business Ethics* 159 (2019) 39.

Pirson, Michael, et al. "Social Innovation and the Future of Business and Business Education." *Humanistic Management Journal* 4 (2020) 1–6.

Pirson, Michael, et al. "Dignity and the Process of Social Innovation: Lessons from Social Entrepreneurship and Transformative Services for Humanistic Management." *Humanistic Management Journal* 4 (2019) 1–29.

Pius XI. *On Reconstruction of the Social Order: Quadragesimo Anno.* http://w2.vatican.va/content/pius-xi/en/encyclicals/documents/hf_p-xi_enc_19310515_quadragesimo-anno.html.

Pontifical Council for Justice and Peace. *Compendium of the Social Doctrine of the Church.* http://www.vatican.va/roman_curia/pontifical_councils/justpeace/documents/rc_pc_justpeace_doc_20060526_compendio-dott-soc_en.html.

———. "Towards Reforming Financial and Monetary Systems in the Context of Global Public Authority." http://www.vatican.va/roman_curia/pontifical_councils/justpeace/documents/rc_pc_justpeace_doc_20111024_nota_en.html.

Porter, Michael E. *Competitive Advantage: Creating and Sustaining Superior Performance.* New York: Free, 1985.

Porter, Michael E., and Mark R. Kramer. "Creating Shared Value." *Harvard Business Review,* January 1, 2011. https://hbr.org/2011/01/the-big-idea-creating-shared-value.

Post, James E. "Assessing the Nestlé Boycott: Corporate Accountability and Human Rights." *California Management Review* 27 (1985) 113–31.

Powell, Ashlea. "How IDEO Designers Persuade Companies to Accept Change." *Harvard Business Review,* May 17, 2016. https://hbr.org/2016/05/how-ideo-designers-persuade-companies-to-accept-change.

Prieb, Tyler. "Global Missions Needs the Tools of Design." *Tyler Prieb* (blog). https://tylerprieb.com/global-missions-needs-the-tools-of-design.

Bibliography

———. "The Theology of Ministry Design." *Tyler Prieb* (blog). https://tylerprieb.com/the-theology-of-ministry-design/.

Rahner, Karl. *Grace in Freedom*. New York: Herder and Herder, 1969.

Reyes, Gaston de los, et al. "Beyond the 'Win-Win': Creating Shared Value Requires Ethical Frameworks." *California Management Review* 59 (2017) 142–67.

Richter, Ulf Henning. "Drivers of Change: A Multiple Case Study on the Process of Institutionalization of Corporate Responsibility among Three Multinational Companies." *Journal of Business Ethics* 102 (2011) 261–79.

Rieger, Joerg. *No Rising Tide: Theology, Economics, and the Future*. Minneapolis: Fortress, 2009.

Rittel, Horst, and Melvin Webber. "Dilemmas in a General Theory of Planning." *Policy Sciences* 4 (1973) 155–69.

Ruttenberg, Danya. "Let's Talk about Trauma, Terror, and the Golden Calf for a Moment, Shall We? And Of Course, What Is Happening Today." *Life Is a Sacred Text*, April 4, 2022. https://lifeisasacredtext.substack.com/p/the-trauma-of-the-golden-calf.

Ryan, John A. *Distributive Justice: The Right and Wrong of Our Present Distribution of Wealth*. London: Forgotten, 2017.

———. *Economic Justice: Selections from Distributive Justice and a Living Wage*. Louisville, KY: Westminster John Knox, 1996.

Sadowski, Dennis. "Business Leaders Explore Ways to Carry Catholic Values to the Office." *National Catholic Reporter*, September 30, 2014. https://www.ncronline.org/news/parish/business-leaders-explore-ways-carry-catholic-values-office.

Sanchez, Rachel Joyce Marie O. "Where Is Women's Wisdom in the Life of the Church? A Feminist Perspective on the International Theological Commission's '*Sensus Fidei* in the Life of the Church.'" *Journal of Feminist Studies in Religion* 32 (2016) 27–43.

Sapiro, Virginia. "Interdisciplinary and Collaborative Teaching at the UW-Madison: Overcoming Barriers to Vitality in Teaching and Learning." University of Wisconsin–Madison, March 2004. https://blogs.bu.edu/vsapiro/files/2017/10/SapiroInterdisciplinary.pdf.

Satell, Greg. "Why 'Move Fast and Break Things' Doesn't Work Anymore." *Harvard Business Review*, December 10, 2019. https://hbr.org/2019/12/why-move-fast-and-break-things-doesnt-work-anymore.

Schlag, Martin, and Domènec Melé, eds. *A Catholic Spirituality for Business: The Logic of Gift*. Washington, DC: Catholic University of America Press, 2019.

Second Vatican Council. *Pastoral Constitution on the Church in the Modern Word: Gaudium et Spes*. http://www.vatican.va/archive/hist_councils/ii_vatican_council/documents/vat-ii_const_19651207_gaudium-et-spes_en.html.

Segundo, Juan Luis. *Grace and the Human Condition*. Maryknoll, NY: Orbis, 1973.

Siriattakul, Parinya, et al. "The Mediating Role of Employee Engagement between Team and Co-worker Relation, Work Environment, Training and Development, and Employee Performance." *International Journal of Psychosocial Rehabilitation* 23 (2019) 853–54.

Stanley, Vincent. "Meaningful Work in a Time of Crisis." In *Working Alternatives: American and Catholic Experiments in Work and Economy*, edited by John C. Seitz and Christine Firer Hinze, 280–303. Fordham: Fordham University Press, 2020.

Starik, Mark. "Should Trees Have Managerial Standing? Toward Stakeholder Status for Non-human Nature." *Journal of Business Ethics* 14 (1995) 207–17.

Bibliography

Stolle, Bethany. "Theology and Design: What Is Design Thinking?" http://ministryincubators.com/wp-content/uploads/2018/01/Session1_WhatIsDesignThinking_Handout.pdf.

Subramaniam, Vanmala. "A Look into Nestle's Controversial Water Bottling Business in Canada." *Vice*, September 30, 2016. https://www.vice.com/en_ca/article/zn85qw/a-look-into-nestles-controversial-water-bottling-business-in-canada.

Sustainability Accounting Standards Board. "About Us." https://sasb.ifrs.org/about/

Sylla, Ndongo Samba, and David Clement Leye. *The Fair Trade Scandal: Marketing Poverty to Benefit the Rich*. Athens, OH: Ohio University Press, 2014.

The Synod of Bishops for the Pan-Amazon. *Final Document of the Amazon Synod*. http://www.sinodoamazonico.va/content/sinodoamazonico/en/documents/final-document-of-the-amazon-synod.html.

Tan, Jonathan Yun-ka. "Theologizing at the Service of Life: The Contextual Theological Methodology of the Federation of Asian Bishops' Conferences (FABC)." *Gregorianum* 81 (2000) 541–75.

Taneja, Hemant. "The Era of 'Move Fast and Break Things' Is Over." *Harvard Business Review*, January 22, 2019. https://hbr.org/2019/01/the-era-of-move-fast-and-break-things-is-over.

Townes, Emilie M. *Womanist Ethics and the Cultural Production of Evil*. New York: Palgrave Macmillan, 2007.

Traina, Cristina L. H. "'This Is the Year': Narratives of Structural Evil." *Journal of the Society of Christian Ethics* 37 (2017) 3–19.

Wafula. "Nestlé to Train Nandi, Bungoma Coffee Farmers." *Daily Nation*, June 11, 2019. https://www.nation.co.ke/business/Nestle-targets-18000-coffee-farmers-in-training-plan/996-5153110-12qh6r6/index.html.

Wallace, Cynthia R. "Empathy Is Both Better and Worse Than We Think." *Sojourners*, February 3, 2021. https://sojo.net/articles/empathy-both-better-and-worse-we-think.

Werhane, Patricia H. "Globalization, Mental Models, and Decentering Stakeholder Approaches." In *Systems Thinking and Moral Imagination: Rethinking Business Ethics*, edited by David J. Bevan and Regina W. Wolfe, 129–44. Eminent Voices in Business Ethics. Switzerland: Springer International, 2019.

———. "Moral Imagination and Systems Thinking." *Journal of Business Ethics* 38 (2002) 33–42.

Whitehead, James D. *Method in Ministry: Theological Reflection and Christian Ministry*. Rev. ed. Kansas City: Sheed & Ward, 1995.

Whitehead, James D., and Evelyn E. Whitehead. "Attending to the Experience of Injustice." In *Method in Ministry: Theological Reflection and Christian Ministry*, edited by James D. Whitehead, 128–29. London: Sheed & Ward, 1995.

Woodward, David G. "Is the Natural Environment a Stakeholder? Of Course It Is (No Matter What the Utilitarians Might Say)!" Conference Presentation presented at the Critical Perspectives on Accounting Conference, 2002. https://eprints.soton.ac.uk/36647/.

World Synod of Catholic Bishops. "Justice in the World." https://www.cctwincities.org/wp-content/uploads/2015/10/Justicia-in-Mundo.pdf.

www.ingramcontent.com/pod-product-compliance
Lightning Source LLC
Chambersburg PA
CBHW050821160426
43192CB00010B/1845